Instant Discussions

Richard MacAndrew
with Ron Martínez

United Kingdom • United States • Australia • Canada • Mexico • Singapore • Spain

THOMSON
™
HEINLE

Instant Discussions, *Richard MacAndrew, Ron Martínez*

Publisher: *Chris Wenger*
Project Manager: *Jimmie Hill*
Director ESL/ELT Marketing: *Amy Mabley*
Manufacturing Coordinator: *Mary Beth Hennebury*
Sr. Production Editor: *Sally Cogliano*

Production Editor: *Tan Jin Hock*
Cartoon Researcher: *Jimmie Hill*
Illustrator: *Anna Macleod*
Cover Designer: *Anna Macleod*
Printer: *Seng Lee Press*

Printed in Singapore.
  2 3 4 5 6 7 8 9 10   06 05

For more information contact:
Thomson Learning
50/51 Bedford Row
London
WC1R 4LR
United Kingdom

or

Heinle
25 Thomson Place
Boston, MA 02210
USA

or you can visit our Internet site at
http://www.heinle.com

Permission to photocopy

The authors

Richard MacAndrew has taught in Finland, Sweden, Malaysia and the UK. He is now a full-time writer of ELT materials, but gets back into the classroom whenever possible. He has previously written *English Observed* (Heinle/LTP 1992), *Taboos and Issues* (Heinle/LTP 2001), and has also had work published by OUP, CUP and Macmillan Heinemann.

Ron Martínez, a native of San Francisco, is an EFL author, teacher and teacher trainer with extensive classroom experience in the United States, Spain and Brazil. He is currently working as a materials developer for CEL-LEP schools in São Paulo, Brazil. He is the author of *Conversation Lessons* for Heinle/LTP.

The authors would like to thank Michael Lewis, whose enthusiasm started this project, and Jimmie Hill, who kept things together to the end.

Disclaimer

The publishers and authors would like to make it clear that any views expressed are solely to provoke classroom discussion and do not reflect their own personal views or attitudes. Teachers are encouraged to refer to the Introduction and unit-by-unit notes for guidance on handling this material.

Acknowledgements
Cartoons reproduced by kind permission of:
Punch Ltd.: *the cartoons in units 1, 3, 9, 14, 19, 23, 29, 33, 34*
Private Eye: *the cartoons in units 4, 6, 11, 13, 18, 21, 22, 27, 31*
The Oldie: *the cartoons in units 2, 5, 10, 15, 26, 40*

ISBN: 0-7593-9630-2

Introduction

Introduction

Instant Discussions is a photocopiable resource of 40 discussion lessons for teachers to take into the classroom with minimal preparation. The material is a resource from which teachers and classes can select topics of interest. The topics chosen occur widely in everyday life and fall into a number of different categories:

1. The unusual
These include: *Incredible stories* and *Neighbours from hell*.

2. A fresh look at old topics
We have tried to approach traditional classroom topics from a new angle. For example, in a unit on the environment we ask, 'Who really cares about the environment? Is it really that important to save a two-centimetre-long lizard that a year ago nobody knew existed?'

3. Ethical problems
Unlike *Taboos and Issues*, the sister volume to this book, which looks almost exclusively at controversial and sensitive issues, *Instant Discussions* deals with very few such topics. However, we have included some for those teachers whose classes like to get their teeth into a tough topic. For example, we examine the problems of IVF treatment for childless couples in *A matter of birth and death*; we discuss prayer in *The power of prayer*. These subjects should be approached with care and used only with classes of sufficient maturity and sensitivity.

4. The topical
We have tried to include some issues which would not have been included in older coursebooks: internet dating in *The dating game*; the use of mobile phones in *I'm on the train*.

5. 'Different' topics
These topics are different from the 'unusual' since they are quite likely to feature in everyday conversation. However, they are topics that are not often found in standard coursebooks. For example, *To tip or not to tip?* and *Royalty*.

How a unit is organised

Most units follow this pattern:

left-hand page: introductory discussion and one or more short texts

right-hand page: language work and further discussion

The left-hand page usually provides the basic material for a lesson, while the right-hand page provides extension or follow-up work.

Methodology

This material is designed for both experienced and less experienced teachers. You should note that a few topics are of a controversial or sensitive nature and teachers should be careful when using these.

Teacher's notes have been kept to a minimum and comprise only a few short notes, warnings about particularly sensitive units, the answers and occasional extra ideas.

Units usually begin with a lead-in discussion to introduce the topic. Ask students to think silently about the questions for a few minutes before they start talking. We recommend that students work in pairs or small groups throughout the initial stages of a lesson so that they get the maximum opportunity to participate. During pair work or group work you can move around the class monitoring what is happening . You can help out with language where necessary and decide whether and how a topic should be opened out for discussion by the whole class. As a teacher, you should obviously remain neutral throughout any discussion, allowing students to express their own views and reach their own conclusions. With the more sensitive topics in this collection it is important that students are not pressured in any way into discussing or revealing things about themselves with which they are in any way unhappy. The material obviously encourages students to express their views and experiences. However, a student who wishes to remain silent must have their right to do so respected.

Using the internet

Because we have chosen topical and popular subjects, it will almost always be easy to find related material by a quick search of the internet. You can easily supplement your lessons with such material.

Richard MacAndrew
Ron Martínez

Contents

Teenage rebellion

Discussion

Look at this questionnaire about what you, and people you know, did, or do, as teenagers. Tick the appropriate boxes.

You	A friend	Someone in your family	
☐	☐	☐	wore an earring or earrings.
☐	☐	☐	wore rings on other parts of their body.
☐	☐	☐	always wore black.
☐	☐	☐	wore very unusual clothes.
☐	☐	☐	had an unusual hairstyle.
☐	☐	☐	started smoking before they were 14.
☐	☐	☐	dropped out of school or college.

Compare your answers in pairs. In what other ways do young people express rebellion?

Reading

1. Read the following news item which appeared in *The Daily Telegraph*. Discuss the questions below in pairs:

Schoolgirl Ashley Wallace, 16, was furious when the headmaster of her school, Neil Watts, 50, ordered the school photographers to change the colour of her hair from pink to brown in the final prints of the official school photographs.

1. Why do you think the headmaster wanted the colour of Ashley's hair changed?
2. Why do you think Ashley was furious?
3. Why do you think Ashley dyed her hair pink?

2. Now read the views of Ashley and the headmaster and answer the questions below.

ASHLEY'S VIEW

I couldn't believe it when I realised what they had done to me. I was so annoyed that I went straight to the headmaster and complained.

My hair was a mousy brown and it looked ridiculous because you could still see all the pink through it. All of my friends were asking what I had done to my hair. I was just fuming.

The school should have given me the option either to be in the photo and have my hair airbrushed or not be in it. If I had been given the choice, I would rather not have been in it at all. One thing is certain – there is no way I am going to change my hair colour now!

THE HEADMASTER'S VIEW

We have been trying to resolve the issue of Ashley's pink hair since before Christmas. Initially, we were assured that she would return it to the natural colour over the holiday but since Christmas her hair has remained pink.

Our code of conduct clearly states that pupils are expected to bring credit upon themselves by their appearance and we do not feel that pink hair fulfils this requirement.

Despite this we have acted very reasonably. We have not excluded Ashley from school and we have allowed her to attend normal lessons in the final year of her exams.

We also allowed her to be in the photograph for the whole year group. However, we feel strongly that, as the photograph is a record for the school, Ashley's hair colour does not bring credit upon the other pupils and the school. Therefore, we asked the photographic company to tone down the hair colour in the photograph.

1. Why was Ashley furious?
2. What did she think the school should have done?
3. How long had Ashley had pink hair?
4. How did the headmaster feel about her hair?
5. In what ways did he feel the school had been reasonable towards her?

Discussion

Discuss these questions in pairs or small groups:

1. Who do you think is right – Ashley or the headmaster? Why?
2. Are there any better solutions to the problem of Ashley's hair? What are they?
3. If a 16-year-old arrived at school one morning with pink hair in your country:
   what would her friends say?
   what would her teachers say?
   what would the headteacher say?

Language

1. Ashley uses quite informal language. Find the informal expressions she uses to say these more formal phrases:

a. *I sought an immediate meeting with the head.*
b. *I was extremely upset.*
c. *I have no intention of …*

2. Find the more formal expressions the head uses to say these less formal phrases:

a. *We've been trying to sort out …*
b. *First, we were told …*
c. *pupils ought to show a bit of self-respect …*
d. *We haven't thrown Ashley out of the school.
… we've let her come to school as usual …*

3. Put these sentences into more formal English:

1. I was so cross that he did not sort out the problem of the timetable.
2. There's no way I'm going to let him into my classes again.
3. I'm going straight to the boss.
4. We've decided that your son should not come back to this school.
5. First, I'd like to make it clear to you that classes will take place as normal.

"I think he's swallowed his father."

Discussion

Discuss these situations in pairs:

1. Jessica wears old black clothes all the time. She has rings in her ears and her eyebrows. She has dyed her hair black and uses black eye make-up. Her brother is getting married soon. Her mother wants her to wear something different for the wedding. Should she? And if so, what?

2. You have invited your neighbours and their children to a party at your house. Their 15-year-old son arrives wearing shorts, black tights, an orange T-shirt and has a number of chains round different parts of his body. Should you say anything about the way he is dressed? If so, what?

3. Mark's 18-year-old son usually has shoulder-length hair. Mark has insisted that he gets it cut before a family wedding. He arrives at the church with short hair – dyed bright green. What should Mark say or do?

4. Jenny is 16 and gets good results at school. She wants to leave school at the end of term, get a job (any job will do), and move into a flat with three of her girlfriends. Should her parents persuade her to stay on at school? If so, how?

5. Mary accidentally finds cigarettes and beer hidden in her 14-year-old daughter's bedroom. Should she say anything to her? If so, what?

Have these or any similar situations happened to you or anyone you know?

Compare your answers with other groups.

Protest

Some forms of popular music are influential in shaping teenagers' opinions. Look at these quotations and discuss the questions:

'Your sons and your daughters are beyond your command. Your old road is rapidly agin'.'
(Bob Dylan, The Times They Are A-changin', 1964.)

Are these lines relevant today?
Do all teenagers rebel against their parents?
Do you know any who haven't?

'If I'm more of an influence to your son as a rapper than you are as a father, you got to look to yourself as a parent.'
(Ice Cube, in an interview in 1990.)

Do you agree with this or not? Why?
Is there anything parents can do to stop their teenage children rebelling?

Incredible stories

Discussion

Work in small groups. Discuss these questions:
1. What is the most extraordinary true story you have heard or read recently?
2. Who was involved and what happened?
Compare your answers with other groups.

Reading

Read the stories below. Six are true and two are false. Decide with a partner which are which.

MAN EVICTED
A German man was evicted from his flat in Berlin because he laughed too much and too loudly. Rudi Bauer, 52, was forced to leave his home after neighbours complained.

NEW UNIVERSITY COURSES
New degree courses on offer at some of Britain's universities include: golf at Birmingham, theology and water resources at Oxford Brookes, philosophy and waste management at Northampton University College, and watersports studies at Southampton Institute.

PEA SHOOTING CONTROVERSY
This year's World Pea Shooting Championships – contestants shoot dried peas at a soft clay target – take place in Witcham, Cambridgeshire. It is hoped there will not be a repetition of last year's controversy when the winner used a laser guidance system.

TALKING WASHING MACHINES
Electrolux has just announced the launch of its first talking washing machine, which has gone on sale in India. The company is also developing a cooker which will learn how cooks like to cook their food.

FREE SEX CHANGE
The city of San Francisco has decided to provide free sex change operations for employees who have worked for the city for at least one year. Opponents say the measure will just encourage people to apply for jobs with the city in order to get a free sex change.

STUCK IN THE AIR
A woman on a Scandinavian Airlines flight became stuck to a lavatory seat when she used the vacuum flush while still seated. She was freed when the plane landed.

SAVE THE BEST TILL LAST
Most people think that an index is a boring, but sometimes useful, bit at the back of a book. But it is much more than that. The British Library has just published a collection of the 71 best indexes of all time – from 1427 to the present day.

BACK INTO THE RECORDS
Grant Melville, 45, has walked into the record books backwards! He climbed Ben Nevis, the highest mountain in Britain, making the whole ascent backwards. The climb and descent took 15 hours 37 minutes.

Discussion

Discuss these questions in small groups:

1. Which story do you find most extraordinary? Why?
2. Do any similar things happen in your country? For example, have people been evicted from their homes for unusual reasons? Are there any university courses you consider strange? Are there any unusual world championships held in your country?
3. Think about the people involved in each story. What do you think are the reasons behind their actions?

Language 1

1. Complete the table below with words from the texts above:

VERB	NOUN
manage	management
contest	. . . .
repeat	. . . .
guide	. . . .
launch	. . . .
operate	. . . .
oppose	. . . .
collect	. . . .
ascend	. . . .
descend	. . . .

2. Think of other nouns, as well as the words from the text, which could go in the second column.

Language 2

Complete the text below using the correct forms of words from the exercise above:

SECOND VICTORY FOR LANCASHIRE

This year's hill climbing . . . . (1) between the University of South Yorkshire and Lancashire College of Education took place last Saturday at Whernside. Teams from each university were expected to complete the . . . . (2) and . . . . (3) of both Whernside and Ingleborough, ... (4) badges from a number of checkpoints on the way. Lancashire College of Education . . . . (5) last year's success, winning by four minutes. Alex Bolton, ... (6) of the Lancashire team, said afterwards: "We would like to congratulate our . . . . (7) on a hard fought race. It was a narrow victory. We would also like to thank our coach, Helen Wright, whose . . . . (8) and support has been an important factor in our victory."

Discussion

Work in pairs or small groups. Make up stories to go with three or four of the following headlines. Write a paragraph or two for each story. Make the stories as unusual as you can! Then compare your answers with those of other groups.

1. **NEW FUEL FOR CARS OF THE FUTURE**

2. **ROBBERY WITH LOVE AND PEACE**

3. **COMPUTERS THAT THINK**

4. **THE SHORTEST CD EVER**

5. **MAN BITES DOG**

6. **TWO NEW OLYMPIC SPORTS**

7. **NEW NATIONAL FLAG APPROVED**

8. **STRANGE MEETING IN SAHARA DESERT**

"And don't forget your optician's appointment."

Naming and shaming

Discussion

1. Match the following punishments to the definitions below:

1. a fine
2. a prison sentence
3. a suspended prison sentence
4. community service
5. tagging
6. the death penalty
7. corporal punishment
8. solitary confinement

a. you go to prison
b. you have to pay money as a punishment
c. you have to spend some time working for the local community
d. you are beaten or punished physically in some way
e. you are killed (for example, by hanging, electrocution, or some other way)
f. you can live at home, but if you commit another crime, you will be sent to prison
g. you are kept in prison on your own – away from other prisoners
h. you have an electronic device fitted to your body so that the police always know where you are

2. Discuss these questions in pairs:

1. Which of the above punishments are used in your country?
2. What other punishments are used?
3. What is the reasoning behind each different type of punishment?
4. Which punishment is the most effective? Which is the least effective?

Reading

Read the article below and then answer these questions:

1. What sentences were given for a) shoplifting b) drunk driving?
2. What does one woman think are the benefits of these sentences?

LET THE PUNISHMENT FIT THE CRIME!

In a number of courts in the US 'naming and shaming' is working. If you are found guilty of shoplifting, you may expect a fine or a short prison sentence, but you might actually receive a totally different punishment. You could have to spend a couple of weeks walking up and down the street outside the store you stole from, carrying a sign that reads: 'I am a thief. Do not steal! This could be you.'

This somewhat eccentric sentencing policy has an effect. Consider the drunk driver forced to confront the consequences of his actions every week for five years. His sentence was to write a one-dollar cheque every Friday to the man whose daughter he ran over. At the bottom of each cheque he had to write 'For causing the death of your daughter.'

Shamed offenders often do not like their sentences – and that is the point. 'Shame makes you stop and think,' says a woman with a recent conviction for theft. 'It gave me humility, which helped me. And if other people see the sign, maybe they'll think twice before they commit a crime.'

The only question is: how far will we go down this road? Will each town revive its public stocks? Will we soon be going along to throw tomatoes and rotten eggs at convicted criminals? And is this a step forward or a step back?

Discussion

Look at these statements about the article you read. Decide if you agree or disagree.

1. I don't think humiliation is a good way to punish people. In schools we don't humiliate children any longer when they misbehave. We shouldn't do it to adults either.

2. The punishment for the drunk driver is not enough. It's a clever idea, but this man should also be spending a substantial time in prison.

3. I think the punishment for shoplifting is far too lenient. A few weeks in prison would be much more effective.

4. These types of punishment are a step back towards the middle ages. Surely civilisation has progressed since then. What will these people want next? Public hangings?

Compare your answers in pairs or small groups.

Language

Find these words and expressions in the text above:

sentence
cause the death of …
prison

an offender
commit a crime
a criminal

conviction
a fine
find someone guilty of …

Complete the text below using appropriate forms of the words and phrases above:

Darren Jackson, 31, of Oxford Road, Abingdon was . . . . (1) yesterday of . . . . (2) Abigail Hunt while driving under the influence of drink. Judge Barbara Mowat . . . . (3) Mr Jackson to a £1000 . . . . (4) and three years in . . . . (5) saying: "You have . . . . (6) a very serious crime. And what is worse, you have a previous, similar . . . . (7). You may think you are unlucky. I think you are a shameless . . . . (8). I am giving you a harsh sentence in the hope that it will be a warning to other potential . . . . (9)."

Correct the wrong endings to this sentence:

He should be   locked.
                     put in bars.
                     sent in prison.

Discussion

In an effort to stop petty crime, your government wants to develop a new and radical system of punishments for dealing with minor criminals. Work in pairs and devise suitably imaginative punishments for people who:

1. steal stationery and pens from their employer
2. break the speed limit when driving
3. leave a restaurant without paying the bill
4. pick pockets
5. park illegally
6. steal mobile phones

For example:

People who steal mobile phones should:
– be made to work in a call centre for two years.
– spend one day a week for a year cleaning public phone boxes.
– be fitted with an electronic device that blocks mobile phone signals for a distance of ten metres from the wearer.

Compare your answers with other groups.

"Excuse me, madam,
but I have reason to suspect . . ."

Neighbours from hell

Discussion

Tell a partner if you have ever had any of the following problems with a neighbour:

1. They were making too much noise.
2. They regularly held wild parties.
3. They left smelly rubbish on the street.
4. They lit bonfires in their garden.
5. They threw rubbish on to your property.
6. They kept dangerous animals.

Tell your partner what happened and how you reacted. What would you do if a neighbour did any of the things above?

Reading

Read the newspaper article and answer the questions below. What five things do the Thompsons say that Miss Hill has done to annoy them?

"How are you getting on with your neighbours now?"

SHE ATE OUR FISH!

Moving to Blades Farm deep in the Oxfordshire countryside three years ago should have been a dream come true for Bill and Glenda Thompson. But it was not to be. Oxford County Court heard yesterday how arguments with their neighbour, Sharon Hill, 63, had led to a cycle of hatred and violence.

At first the Thompsons found Miss Hill friendly, if slightly eccentric. However, a shared driveway to both their houses soon led to the first disagreement. Miss Hill became increasingly unhelpful about keeping the drive clear, often leaving her car parked there and forcing the Thompsons to carry bags of shopping 50 metres to their house.

This was followed by a dispute over land. When Miss Hill replaced a fence between the two properties, the Thompsons accused her of stealing a strip of land from them. A few weeks later she cut down a tree which the Thompsons allege was theirs. She then bought a large Alsatian dog, which Mrs Thompson claims has attacked her on more than one occasion.

"She knows I hate dogs," said Mrs Thompson. "She doesn't need one and only bought it to frighten me." The last straw came when some fish disappeared from a pond in the Thompsons' garden. "We thought they could have been stolen by a cat or a bird," said Mr Thompson, "but that evening she had a barbecue in her garden and she kept shouting to us that she'd got some lovely fish. I know they were our fish. She's completely mad."

The Thompsons want to move but are unable to sell their house while the feud continues. They are now seeking £65,000 compensation from Miss Hill for the loss in value of their home. "I can't understand what the problem is," protests Miss Hill. "I haven't done anything wrong. The Thompsons used to be quite friendly but now they're just causing trouble."

The case continues.

Discussion

Discuss these questions in pairs or small groups:

How do you think Miss Hill might try and show she has done nothing wrong?

If the Thompsons are correct, how do you think the judge should deal with the situation?

If you were in a situation like the Thompsons, would you go to court? Or would you try and deal with the matter in a different way?

Language

1. Study this sentence and answer the questions below:

Arguments had led to a cycle of hatred and violence.

a. Find three other words meaning 'arguments'.

. . . .

. . . .

. . . .

b. Which of these words would you use about arguments between families or countries that last for a long time?

2. Study this sentence and answer the questions below:

The Thompsons accused her of stealing a strip of land.

a. Find three other verbs which mean 'to say that you think something is true'.

. . . .

. . . .

. . . .

b. Which of these verbs is often used of someone defending themselves?

c. Why are these verbs often used in newspaper articles about court cases?

Discussion

Discuss these questions in small groups:

1. What laws are there in your country governing relations between neighbours?
2. What happens in the following situations?
   a. you want to build an extension on your house.
   b. your neighbour puts up a new fence and 'steals' a few centimetres of your garden.
   c. you want to put up a shed in your garden.
   d. your neighbour has a dog that barks a lot during the day.
   e. you want to go on your neighbour's land to repair your house.
   f. your neighbour paints his front door a horrible shade of bright orange.
   g. your neighbour decides to keep pigs in his garden.
   h. a tree in your neighbour's garden starts to block off a lot of light from your house and garden.

Expressions

Complete the following common expressions from the text:

1. It should have been a . . . . . . come true.
2. It soon . . . . . . to the first disagreement.
3. They had a dispute . . . . . . land.
4. It attacked them on more than one . . . .
5. That was the . . . . . . straw.
6. They just . . . . . . trouble.

Note: people who cause trouble are known as *troublemakers*.

Questionnaire

Answer the questionnaire below:

1. It is two o'clock in the morning and there is a very noisy party going on in a flat across the street. You have to get up at six to catch a plane. Do you:
a. roll over and keep trying to get some sleep?
b. call the police?
c. go and join the party? (Well, missing four hours' sleep isn't too bad!)
d. do something else?

2. The new baby in the house next door often cries in the night. That's not a problem. What wakes you up is the father shouting at the baby. Do you:
a. ring social services and report him?
b. call the police and tell them?
c. talk to the baby's mother and find out if everything's OK?
d. do something else?

3. Your neighbour's garden is a mess. It's like a jungle – full of rubbish and rats. Do you:
a. ask him politely to do something about it?
b. report him to the local council?
c. wait till he goes on holiday and then buy some powerful weedkiller and rat poison?
d. do something else?

4. You are having a party in your garden one sunny summer's afternoon and your neighbour, who was invited to the party but didn't come, decides to light a bonfire so that the smoke blows over your garden. Do you:
a. take your guests inside and ignore your neighbour's behaviour?
b. go round and ask him to put it out?
c. find your garden hose, lean over the fence and put it out yourself?
d. do something else?

What's in a name?

Discussion

Write down your five favourite and five least favourite names for boys and girls:

Favourite boys' names: . . . .

Boys' names you don't like: . . . .

Favourite girls' names: . . . .

Girls' names you don't like: . . . .

Compare your answers in small groups and discuss why you like or dislike these names.

Reading

Read the text below about where names come from. Think of some examples of names in your language from as many of the sources listed below as possible. Compare your answers in pairs.

Where do names come from?

Traditional names

Traditional names are those handed down from long ago through a particular culture. These names may once have had a meaning, but that will now be a minor factor in their choice and use. From Germany there are names like Frederick and Matilda; from Scandinavia Ingrid and Gustav; from Slavic culture Pavel and Kazimiera.

Scriptural and religious names

Many names are scriptural names. From Christian scriptures Matthew and Mary are examples from the New Testament; Jacob and Rebecca from the Old Testament. Islam gives us many forms of the name Muhammad, and of his descendants, for example Omar and Fatima. Ibrahim and Mariam are examples from the Muslim scripture, the Koran. Hinduism brings us Krishna and Sita, the names of traditional Hindu deities.

Names from mythology and literature

Daphne and Hector are examples of names which derive from Greek mythology; Arthur and Elaine from Arthurian legend. Shakespeare gave us Cordelia, and Jessica.

Days and position in the family

These concepts are particularly common in African names. For example, the name Esi means 'Sunday' and 'Kunto' means third child. These ideas are unusual in western culture, although the American actress Tuesday Weld is a notable exception.

Family names

These have become more commonly used as first names in recent times: for example, *Cameron* Mackintosh and *Beverley* Sills.

Vocabulary words

Many new names are also created from ordinary words. Jade (Jade Jagger) and River (River Phoenix) are well-known current examples.

Variations

And, of course, the total is considerably increased by the number of variations of each name that can be created. Robert can also be Rob, Robbie, Bob or Bobby; Jessica can be Jess or Jessie. And boys' names can be made into girls' names. Robert becomes Roberta, Nicolas becomes Nicola or Nicole or Nicky or Nikki.

Discussion

Discuss these questions with a partner, then report to the whole class:

1. Tell a partner the origin of your names. What about your parents' names?
2. Is there a tradition in your family of using names of grandparents for children?
3. If you have children, why did you choose the names you did?

The origin of names

Work in pairs. Match the names on the left with their origins on the right:

Names	Origin
Cara	Slavic
Andrew	Celtic/Gaelic
Pavel	Japanese
Fatima	Welsh
Tokala	Vietnamese
Kunto	British
Meredith	African
Duc	Greek
Washi	Native American
Chloe	Arabic

Some names have special meanings. For example, Andrew can mean *brave, little one, moral, good, eagle,* and *fox.* Cara can mean *sweet melody, daughter of the prophet,* and *third child.* Does your name have a special meaning?

"Yes, we are Mr and Mrs Smith, but we want to book in as Mr Pearson and Miss Jones, just to make it more exciting."

Discussion

Discuss these questions in small groups:

1. Which first names are most popular in your country at the moment?
2. Were the same names popular amongst your parents' generation? What names were popular then?
3. Which are more popular in your country – birthdays or name days? What happens on these days?

Language

Here are 8 verbs and 8 adjectives we use to talk about things we do or do not like. Mark them in the following way:

+ like very much   – dislike   o no strong feelings

I love ...	I quite like ...	beautiful	awful
I loathe ...	I don't mind ...	ugly	OK
I hate ...	I adore ...	gorgeous	strong
I'm fond of ...	I detest ...	powerful	pathetic

Work in pairs. Do you like the following names or not? Use the words and phrases above to help you talk about them. For example: *I just love Anastasia. I think it's a beautiful name.*

| Hilda | Bernard | Jemima | Madonna | Roger | Cynthia |
| Arnold | Dolores | Gwyneth | Russell | Wayne | Edith |

Discussion

Work in pairs. Decide which of the following ideas you want to discuss. When you are ready, tell the rest of the class what you think:

1. **Changing names:** Everyone knows that Marilyn Monroe's real name was Norma Jean Mortenson. Why did she change it? Why do people change their names? Would you like to change your name? Should women be forced to change their name when they get married?

2. **Nicknames:** The former British Prime Minister, Margaret Thatcher, was known by two nicknames – Maggie or The Iron Lady. It is common for schoolchildren to give each other nicknames such as Ears (for someone with large ears); Curly (for someone with curly hair). What nicknames can you remember from school?

3. **Pet names:** Can you think of typical names in your country for the following animals?

   a dog   a cat   a fish   a pet bird

You've got mail!

Discussion

Answer these questions. Then compare your answers with a partner.

1. Do you send emails? Who to? Why?
2. Do you use the internet? If so, how many times a day? What for?
3. Do you surf the net? Which websites do you visit most often?
4. Do you visit chat rooms? Who do you chat to? What about?
5. Do you have your own website? If so, what is on it?
6. Do any of your friends have their own websites? If so, what are they like?

Reading

Read the text below. Give three reasons why emails are 'dangerous'.

BIG BROTHER IS READING YOUR EMAILS
Emails – so easy, but so dangerous. First of all, how do you write one? Short, like a note or a message? – but that can seem a bit familiar or even impolite. Start 'Dear X' – like a letter? – but that seems a bit formal and long-winded. Because of their speed, emails seem to expect informality, brevity and wit.

But you must be careful. Emails are also a trap. They combine the informality of the spoken word with the legal force of the written word. And unlike real documents you can never really get rid of them. They are always there somewhere in the computer. Increasingly often, they are appearing in court. Cases of divorce, sexual harassment and unfair dismissal have all been decided recently on the evidence of emails that people had written, but not really thought about. One problem is that a joke doesn't always work in an email. People don't always get it. You can put one of these :-) to make sure that people realise something's a joke. Or if it's a rude joke put ;-) But, unless they know you very well, people are just as likely to find it offensive or stupid as they are to find it funny.

Many British companies now have a clear and open policy of monitoring emails. For them it is a direct way to try and avoid claims of sexism, racism and unfair dismissal. For the individual this may seem like an invasion of privacy – but don't be too critical. Admittedly, the policy is there to keep the company out of court, but if it stops you making a fool of yourself as well, it can't be too bad.

True or false?

Read the text above again and mark the following sentences T (true) or F (false):

1. There are no rules about how to write emails.
2. The good thing about emails is that you can delete them so quickly.
3. Emails are a good way of sending jokes.
4. Many British companies now monitor employees' emails.

Discussion

Answer these questions. Then discuss your answers in pairs or small groups.

1. What sort of style do you use when you write emails?
2. Do you reply to emails immediately or do you wait a while and think about what you want to say?
3. Have you ever sent an email that offended someone by mistake?
4. Do you send people jokes by email? What about pictures?
5. Do you print out your emails or do you leave them on the computer?
6. Is it right for companies to monitor their staff's emails? Is this an invasion of privacy?

Language

1. Match the verbs on the left with an appropriate word or phrase on the right:

visit	music
download	a CD
go	online
key in	a website
surf	the internet
burn	a password
switch on	your computer

2. Complete the text below using words or phrases from the exercise above:

When I get home from college, the first thing I do is . . . . (1) my computer, key in my . . . . (2) and . . . . (3) to check my email. Then I log off and start my homework. I don't often . . . . (4) the internet. When I do, I usually . . . . (5) websites that I know – often those of my favourite bands. Sometimes I'll . . . . (6) some new music and maybe . . . . (7) my own CD.

"Can't talk now – I'm chatting."

Discussion

Which of the following is the most serious problem with the internet?

1. Teenagers spending too much time on it.
2. Buying things with a secure system of payment.
3. Children seeing unsuitable material.
4. People using work time to send personal messages.

What do you think should be done about any or all of these problems?

Problem page

Work in pairs or small groups. Look at these problem page letters and discuss the questions below each one.

Letter 1

Dear Anne
I've recently started going out with someone I met through an internet dating site. We're going to start meeting my friends and family soon. Should I tell them how we met? Or should I ask him to lie and say we met in a more conventional way? What do you think?
Amanda

1. Do you have a friend who meets people through an internet dating site? What kind of people use this method of meeting people?
2. What are the advantages and disadvantages of meeting people this way?
3. What advice would you give to Amanda? Why?

Letter 2

Dear Anne
I'm in my final year at college. One of my friends has been copying lots of his final coursework from internet sites. I think he's going to get a really good grade even though he's done none of the work himself. I'm angry about this and wonder if I should tell the college authorities. What do you think?
Mike

1. Do you think there is a difference between using the internet for research and copying large amounts of text from websites?
2. Do you know anyone who has stolen large amounts of text from the internet to use in college coursework? Is this theft?
3. What advice would you give to Mike?

Letter 3

Dear Anne
My teenage son spends lots of time in chatrooms on the internet. I'm worried that I don't know who he's talking to or what he's talking about. What can I do about this?
Tracy

1. What kind of thing do you think Tracy is worried about?
2. Do you think there are any benefits to her son spending so much time in chatrooms?
3. What advice would you give to Tracy?

Price and value

Discussion

What would you normally spend on:

a new shirt	a hi-fi system	a pair of shoes
food for a week	a one-week holiday	a party for your friends

What do you think is a reasonable amount of money to spend on:

a haircut	a wedding	decorating a bedroom
a flat	a car	a nanny/childminder for a week
a coat for a child	a night out	a year's membership of a gym

Compare your answers in pairs or small groups.

Reading

Read the article below and compare what the stars spend with what you thought was reasonable. How do you feel about it? Choose from the options below.

a. I think it's disgusting and wasteful that they spend so much money.

b. They've earned their money. If I was a movie star, I'd do the same.

c. Sometimes it's wasteful, but sometimes they're just doing what they have to to keep in the business.

Do you have a different reaction? If so, what?

THE PRICE OF EVERYTHING, THE VALUE OF NOTHING!

Variety magazine, the American film industry 'bible', recently published the astonishing 'fact' that an American movie star needs £36.65m to maintain a movie-star lifestyle. Figures quoted include £1.5m a year on entertaining; £720,000 a year on hair, make-up and grooming; and £280,000 on holidays.

Celebrity in Britain comes a little cheaper but will still leave most of us gasping. Take celebrity grooming: a visit to a top stylist will cost £125; a personal trainer £695 for 12 sessions (you can't just join the gym at £1,750 a year!). And what about that weekly pedicure and manicure, the legwax, and a Swedish massage every week? It all adds up to about £30,000 a year.

Homes and home life is always the biggest expense. Guy Ritchie and Madonna spent over £5m on their London home; the Beckhams a modest £2.5m for a seven-bedroom mansion in Hertfordshire. Mrs Beckham describes it as 'very cosy'. The Beckhams then spent £3m on refurbishment including £20,000 on fibre optic lights to recreate the night sky in Brooklyn's bedroom; while Madonna had a £200,000 glass kitchen installed. £8m a year to run a house. Cars: well, allow anything up to £150,000 – a Ferrari for Mr Beckham, please. Weddings: Madonna spent £1.5m on hers, whereas the Beckhams' was cheap at only £500,000. Children: don't ask. Hospital fees at the time of the birth at £1-2,000 a night, nannies at £1,000 a week (including the solicitor to make sure they don't sell your story to the papers), and as for children's clothes! A Gucci baby leather jacket is £900.

Then there's clothes, staff, holidays, PR people – all at prices you and I probably wouldn't believe. British movie stars still aren't in the same league as their US counterparts but at £15m a year to keep it all going, they're not doing too badly!

True or false?

Are the following sentences true (T) or false (F) according to the passage above?

1. On average British movie stars spend more on grooming than American movie stars.

2. The Beckhams spent more on redecorating their home than the house itself cost.

3. Gucci baby clothes are not very expensive.

4. On average, American movie stars spend more money maintaining their lifestyle than British movie stars.

Language

Put these adjectives in the correct box:

cheap   valuable   extravagant
pricey   inexpensive   invaluable
expensive   exorbitant   economical

worth/costing a lot   worth/costing a little

Cross out the wrong word in italics to complete these sentences:

1. £2000 a night! – That's an *exorbitant/expensive* price for a hotel.
2. She's so *extravagant/exorbitant*. She bought a painting that cost over £20,000!
3. £18 for a CD – That's a bit *expensive/valuable*, isn't it?
4. You really must get that diamond ring insured. It's very *pricey/valuable*.
5. Give Jim a pay rise. We can't let him leave the company. He's *invaluable/economical*.
6. £12 for an excellent bottle of wine – That's quite *invaluable/inexpensive* really.
7. We had a great meal and it was so *cheap/pricey*. Only £10 per person for three courses.
8. He only paid £25 for his suit! He's very *cheap/economical*.
9. I was going to order a hamburger, but it was £10! I thought that was a bit *pricey/valuable*.

Discussion

Answer these questions. Then compare your answers with a partner.

1. In her will your grandmother leaves you a valuable painting of her grandmother which you have never really liked. What do you do?
   a. put it in the attic, but keep it because it is part of your family history?
   b. hang it in your living room to impress your friends?
   c. sell it because you would like the money?
   d. something else?

2. You win £10,000 in a competition. What do you do?
   a. spend it on a fantastic holiday for you and your partner?
   b. invest it?
   c. use it to start your own business?
   d. something else?

3. You go into your local music store to buy the latest CD by one of your favourite bands. You can buy a normal version of the CD for the usual price; or you can buy a limited edition of the CD signed by all the members of the band, for twice the normal price.
   a. If you were buying a CD for yourself, would you buy the normal version or the limited edition?
   b. If you were buying a birthday present for a friend, would you buy the normal version or the limited edition?

4. Match the following amounts to the items below:

   £28 million   £10,000   £13,500   £1,384,000   £30,000

   a. A pair of pistols owned by George Washington.
   b. A very rare Rolex watch.
   c. A first edition of *Harry Potter and The Philosopher's Stone*, signed by the author.
   d. A Rembrandt painting.
   e. A stage costume worn by Elvis Presley.

Are we all criminals?

Have you committed a crime?

First answer the following questions on your own:

1. Have you ever stolen anything from a shop?
2. Have you ever taken something from your place of work or study – some paper or a pen?
3. Have you ever photocopied something at work or college without permission?
4. Have you ever not paid in a car park when you should have done?
5. Have you ever sent a private email while you were at work or used the office phone?
6. Have you ever kept something that you found?
7. Have you ever not declared something you should have done on your tax form?
8. Have you ever broken any traffic laws – speeding or parking, perhaps?

Now compare your answers with a partner.

Reading

1. Read the two articles and answer these questions:

1. What did Stacy Truman do with the money she found?
2. What did John and Darius Herbert do with the money they found?

CLEANER JAILED

Stacy Truman, 35, a cleaner at the Basingstoke branch of the Mid-West Bank, was jailed for ten months for the theft of £40,000 from the bank. Finding the safe open one morning, Ms Truman took the money in what she described in court as a 'moment of madness'. She then flew to France where she started spending the money. Two days later, stricken with guilt, she returned to Britain and gave herself up to the Basingstoke police, promising to pay back the money she had already spent. The judge said that her crime demanded an immediate prison sentence. Her solicitor described the sentence as harsh and said she would be appealing.

HONESTY PRAISED BY POLICE

Two boys who handed in a supermarket carrier bag containing £1,600 in cash were praised by the police yesterday. John Herbert, 11, and his brother Darius, 8, found the bag in a bush on their way to school and took it to the local police station. Police identified the bag from other contents as belonging to a local councillor. The boys were given a reward of £160, which they are intending to spend on football shirts and computer games.

Discussion

Discuss these questions in pairs or small groups:

1. If the boys had kept the money, would anybody have found out?
2. Do you think their reward was too much, too little, or about right? Why?
3. If the money the boys found had been yours, would you have given them a reward?
4. How did Stacy Truman think she would get away with her crime?
5. Do you think her prison sentence was too lenient, too harsh, or about right? Why?
6. What would you have done with the money in each situation?

Language 1

Match the phrases underlined in the sentences to the meanings in a-f below:

1. A woman <u>answering to</u> the thief's description was caught on CCTV.
2. The police <u>are looking into</u> a number of burglaries in the area.
3. The thieves <u>broke into</u> the warehouse and stole some valuable carpets.
4. We thought he would go to prison, but he <u>got away with</u> a fine.
5. As it was his first offence, the judge <u>let him off</u> with a warning.
6. I thought we'd lost that book, but it <u>turned up</u> in a box in the attic.

a. *enter illegally*
b. *escape with a very light sentence*
c. *investigate*
d. *match*
e. *appear*
f. *let someone go free*

Language 2

Complete this conversation with the correct form of the underlined verbs in 1 above:

A: Have you heard? The police have caught the thieves who . . . . (1) Jack's house.

B: That's great. But it's been ages since the burglary – how did they catch them?

A: Well, the police were . . . . (2) a bank robbery that happened last month. They found a couple of guys who . . . . (3) the description that the bank clerk gave them. So they searched the flat where these guys were living. They didn't find any money from the bank, but unfortunately for these guys a video recorder and a CD player from Jack's house . . . . (4).

B: Wow! What's going to happen now?

A: Well, the thieves are saying that they don't know anything. The stuff was given to them by a friend who's gone to live in Australia.

B: That's not a very good story.

A: No, but I think they may . . . . (5) it. Apparently, the police want to . . . . them . . . . (6) with a warning. They don't think they'll win if the case goes to court.

B: That's terrible. They really should be going to prison. Jack was off work for weeks after it happened.

Discussion

Recent figures in Britain suggest that more than one in five people would not give information about a crime to the police. Numbers varied according to the type of crime. Nearly one in ten said they would not give information – even for a rape or a murder. Almost a third said they would not give details of people using drugs. Would you contact the police if you had information about the following crimes:

1. a murder?
2. a rape?
3. a burglary at a friend's home?
4. a burglary at the home of someone you don't like?
5. young people using drugs in the city centre?
6. the son of a friend who is using drugs?
7. children buying alcohol underage?
8. a shopkeeper selling alcohol to underage children?

Moral dilemmas

Discuss these questions with a partner:

1. You find a carrier bag full of money in a public toilet. Do you:
   a) keep it?
   b) leave it there?
   c) take it to the police?
   d) do something else?

2. You see a friend of yours removing a computer from your place of work/study. Do you:
   a) assume she's stealing it, but say nothing?
   b) assume she's borrowing it and say nothing?
   c) tell the boss/principal?
   d) ask her what she's doing?
   e) do something else?

3. You see someone shoplifting in a supermarket. Do you:
   a) tell one of the assistants?
   b) tell the shoplifter to put it back?
   c) do nothing?
   d) do something else?

4. You discover a phone box that lets you make free international calls. Do you:
   a) call all your friends who live abroad?
   b) tell everyone you know about it?
   c) tell the phone company?
   d) do something else?

Compare your answers with other pairs.

Things that go bump in the night!

Discussion

Discuss these questions in pairs or small groups:

1. Are there any buildings or places near where you live which people believe are haunted? Where are they? In what way are they haunted?
2. Do you know any ghost stories which people believe to be true? If so, tell a partner.
3. Do you believe in ghosts? Why/why not?

Reading

Read the article and answer these questions:

1. What are the Duncans claiming?
2. What does George Deakin say?
3. What does Angela Cooke say?

BUYERS CAN'T SLEEP

A young couple who bought a 300-year-old cottage in Applefield, North Yorkshire are taking the sellers to court because they were not told the property was haunted.

James Duncan, 28, and his wife Betty, 25, are demanding repayment of the £46,000 they paid for the cottage. They claim that they became aware of an 'evil presence' after they moved into the cottage. They also learnt from a number of local people that the cottage had a spooky reputation.

Applefield resident George Deakin, 72, who has lived in the village all his life, remembers his grandfather telling of a boy being strangled in the cottage in the late eighteenth century.

'I didn't believe in ghosts before I lived here,' said Mr Duncan, a university lecturer. 'I thought it was all rubbish – but there is definitely something here. There are sudden changes in temperature and foul, unexplainable smells; things move of their own accord; and we sometimes wake at night with the sensation of hands around our throats. I've been scared stiff at times.'

Angela Cooke, who sold the cottage to the Duncans, said: 'This is complete nonsense. I lived there for ten years. I never saw a ghost and I never heard about any reputation.'

Discussion

Discuss these questions in pairs or small groups:

1. In Britain, if you sell a house, you have to tell the buyers about any important information that might be relevant. Should sellers have to tell buyers if a house has a reputation for being haunted?
2. Is this case about the paranormal or the forces of evil? Or are the Duncans hypersensitive or perhaps just a bit crazy?
3. If you were the judge in the case above, what would you decide? Why?

Language

In the article above James Duncan says: 'I've been scared stiff at times.' Look at the expressions underlined below and mark them in the following way:

  F = The speaker was frightened.   **S = The speaker was just surprised.**

1. When he took it out of the bag, I couldn't believe my eyes.
2. It suddenly charged towards me and gave me the fright of my life.
3. I heard it on the news last night. You could have knocked me down with a feather.
4. I wasn't expecting it at all. I nearly jumped out of my skin.
5. I'll never do that again. It frightened the life out of me.
6. You should have seen their faces. It took them completely by surprise.

With a partner discuss what you think 'it' might refer to in each example.

Discussion

Work in pairs or small groups. Decide which of the following are real and to what extent you feel they really exist:

spaceships from other worlds	ghosts
black magic	the Bermuda Triangle
angels	the Loch Ness Monster
witches	faith healing
extra-sensory perception	fairies
communicating with the dead	crop circles

Compare your answers with other groups or pairs.

"The story goes that he once lived in this house and he hung himself through loneliness, but we just ignore him."

Reading

Read this article and discuss the questions below:

GHOST HUNT

A team of scientists and volunteers led by Dr Richard Wiseman of the University of Hertfordshire has been investigating Edinburgh's ghosts. Only volunteers who knew nothing of Edinburgh's ghostly history were selected, and they were taken both to places that were believed to be haunted and to places with no reports of ghosts at all. A high frequency of unusual experiences was reported in places with a reputation for being haunted. These experiences included: sudden falls in temperature; feelings of being watched; being touched on the face; having one's clothes pulled; and seeing strange figures.

1. Have you heard of investigations like this in your country? Where and when?
2. How would you explain the findings of the investigation?
3. Would you like to take part in such an investigation? Why/Why not?

Read this advertisement and discuss the questions:

HAVE A HAUNTED HOLIDAY!

Take an 18-day tour of the US, stay in haunted hotels and visit spooky places! Put together your own personalised trip chosen from our carefully-compiled list of the most amazing paranormal experiences the US has to offer.

- **Feel the ghosts of Gerald and Diane in the Hotel de la Poste in New Orleans.**
- **Hear the pathetic sighs of Alice in the Hotel Rosario, Orcas Island.**
- **Experience strange happenings in The Logan Hotel, New Hope, Pennsylvania.**
- **Meet face to face the blue-eyed girl in Resurrection Cemetery, Chicago.**

Call 0800-635-5747 and ask for your free 'Haunted Holidays' brochure.

1. Would you go on a holiday like this? Why/Why not?
2. Do you think this tour would be an interesting experience or a waste of money?
3. What sort of people do you think go on holidays like this?
4. Find more holidays like this on the internet.

Living longer

Discussion

Discuss these questions in pairs or small groups:

1. If your great-great-grandparents were still alive, what questions would you like to ask them?
2. Would you like to live to the age of 120? Why/Why not? Make a list of the benefits and disadvantages of having such a long life.

"We're hoping to be recycled."

Reading

Read the text and find the answers to these questions:

1. What do Dr Harris and Professor Baker agree about?
2. What problem do they foresee?

> **DEAD WOOD**
> A recent article in the journal *Science* by Dr John Harris, professor of bioethics at Manchester University, suggests that ageing, and possibly even death, may soon no longer be inevitable, a theory supported by Professor Edwin Baker of the University of New Maldon. Up till now scientists have believed that even if medical science found cures for the major life-threatening diseases, average life expectancy would not be increased beyond 85.
>
> Recent work, however, suggests that genetic engineering could extend that figure much further by reducing the ageing process.
> Such a scenario would have profound implications especially for advanced technological societies. "It is possible that we would have to reconsider the idea of the absolute sanctity of human life," said Dr Baker. "Some form of 'generational cleansing' would undoubtedly be necessary to clear away the dead wood."

Discussion

Discuss these questions in pairs or small groups:

1. What is meant by the expressions 'generational cleansing' and 'to clear away the dead wood'?
2. Do you agree with Dr Baker? Why/Why not?

Language 1

Complete these expressions from the article:

a. medical . . . .

b. . . . . expectancy

c. the ageing . . . .

d. life-. . . . . diseases

e. . . . . engineering

f. the . . . . of human life

Now complete the text below using the expressions.

Hippocrates, who lived in Greece around 400 BC, is often thought of as being the 'father of medicine' so I suppose you could say that he founded . . . . (1). However, it's probably true to say that it wasn't until the nineteenth century that medicine began to have a serious effect on . . . . (2). It was only then that doctors learnt how to deal with a number of . . . . (3) and as a result people began to live longer. Nowadays, of course, ... (4) is one of the latest developments in medicine and I guess it is only a matter of time before scientists discover how to slow down or even halt . . . . (5) as well as treat or prevent a variety of illnesses.

Discussion

Work in pairs or small groups.

In many countries it is usual for elderly people to live with their families. If people start to live to the age of 120, it suggests a situation where five or more generations could be sharing a house. How would you feel if you were living with your husband or wife plus 10 other people:

  your children (aged 2 and 4)
  your parents (45)
  your grandparents (70)
  your great-grandparents (95)
  your great-great-grandparents (120)

Language 2

Look at the verbs in this conditional sentence:

  If people *lived* till they were over 100, we *would have to* build more old folks' homes.

We use the simple past *(lived)* in the conditional clause, then *would have to* in the main clause. Make more sentences like this using these ideas:

1. pay more tax
2. have bigger houses
3. work longer
4. train more nurses and doctors
5. learn to live together

With a partner, decide what *we would have to do* in these areas:

  jobs
  housing
  medical services
  transport
  pensions
  sport
  entertainment

Famous quotes

Work in pairs or small groups to discuss these quotations:

1. '*Life begins at 40.*' *(Walter B. Pitkin)*
   What do you think he means? Do you agree?

2. '*Life, to be sure, is nothing much to lose. But young men think it is, and we were young.*'*(A. E. Housman)*
   Why do you think the writer said this?

3. '*Life is too short to stuff a mushroom.*' *(Shirley Conran)*
   The writer is talking about cooking. What did she mean? Can you finish this sentence in other ways?
   Life is too short to . . . .

4. '*If I'd known I was going to live this long, I'd have taken better care of myself.*' *(Eubie Blake, aged 100)*
   Do you take care of yourself with a view to living longer? If so, how?

Discussion

In some countries when a couple get married, the husband's parents immediately move in with the newly-married couple. There are organisations in these countries which run courses on 'How To Live With Your In-Laws'. Make a list of the advantages and disadvantages of living with your in-laws when you get married.

Giving to charity

Discussion

Discuss these questions with a partner, then compare your answers with others in the class.

1. How much money do you give each year to charity?
   a) nothing   *b) very little*   *c) more than one week's wages*
2. Which charities do you give to?
   a) local charities   *b) national charities*   *c) international charities*
3. If someone is collecting in the street for a charity, how much do you give them?
   a) nothing   *b) just some small change*   *c) a decent amount*
4. Are there any charities you would not give to? Why not?
5. There is a famous saying in English: *Charity begins at home.* What do you think this means? Do you have something similar in your country?

Reading

Read the four texts and answer these questions:

1. Which people do not give to charity?
2. Which person does give to charity?
3. Which person works for a charity?

Pete

No, I don't give to charity. I really don't think I'm that well-off. Sure, we're trying to move house and we're considering moving to a house that's worth a million and a half. But if I look round the school playground when I take my kids to school I'm by no means the richest person there. In fact, I'm probably somewhere in the middle. If I won a million pounds on the Lottery, I'd be pretty disappointed. I mean, a million pounds really doesn't go very far these days, does it? It wouldn't even get us the house we want.

Michelle

Of course I give. How could I not? I have a roof over my head. I have clean water and enough to eat. I can see a doctor whenever I need to. I can read, write, vote, watch television. I have a job. There are people who have none of these things. Of course I give. I have to. It's frightening that there are some people who are not prepared to try and improve the lives of those living in extreme poverty.

Vikki

There are a few high earners who are extremely generous. One very wealthy government minister is reported to have given £47 million to charity last year. JK Rowling, the Harry Potter author, has given the royalties of two books, worth about £8 million, to a charity. But these are exceptions. Figures show that the richest 20 percent of individuals in Britain give less than 1 per cent of their income; the poorest 10 percent give 3 per cent of their income. Overall, one in three people last year gave nothing. Somehow, we fund-raisers have to change these figures.

Brian

We used to be able to rely on the government for things like health care and education and pensions but nowadays we have to pay for these things out of our own pocket. I paid about £40,000 in tax last year and I got nothing back for it – so, no, I don't feel very generous when it comes to giving away my money.

Discussion

Discuss these questions in small groups:

1. What reasons are given by the four people why people do not give to charity? What other reasons do you think people have for not giving? Are these the real reasons?
2. How do you feel about Pete and Brian? Do you think Michelle is caring and generous, or just naive?
3. Do you think men and women have different attitudes to charities?
4. How do you think charities could encourage more people to donate to them?

Discuss these questions with reference to your own country:

5. How many people give to charity?
   a) most   b) very few   c) about one in ten
6. Do people collect money on the streets?
7. Do you have door-to-door collections?
8. How generous is your government to the Third World?

"I'm sorry – we can take your mother's clothes, but not her."

Language

Look at the following underlined expressions from the texts above:

I've got nothing back for it …

… when it comes to giving away my money.

Use the correct form of these phrasal verbs in the sentences:

give back	pay back
give away	get by
give out	get over
get back	give up

1. She's so generous. She's always . . . . money . . . . to good causes.
2. I had to borrow £100 last week, but I . . . . it . . . . . . as soon as I was paid.
3. She's been . . . . leaflets encouraging people to give money to the earthquake fund.
4. I . . . . a couple of hours each week to address envelopes for a children's charity.
5. Charity is all about giving – you shouldn't expect to . . . . . . something . . . .
6. My parents really don't like accepting charity, but they just can't . . . . any longer.
7. He couldn't . . . . the bank so they took away his house.
8. He's never really . . . . the shame of losing his house.

Match four of the verbs with these meanings:

a. recover from   c. distribute

b. manage financially   d. spend time

Discussion

1. Work in small groups. You have won a million pounds to give away to the charity or charities of your choice. You can give it all to one charity or you can divide it up between a maximum of four different ones. Here is the list of charities. Decide how you will divide up the money. Then share your ideas with other groups.

1. a charity doing research into cancer
2. a charity which looks after homeless people in your town
3. a charity for children from poor backgrounds in your country
4. a charity that helps the poor in Africa
5. a charity to train guide dogs for blind people
6. an international AIDS charity
7. a charity for old people in your town
8. a charity for the victims of a recent earthquake in Latin America
9. a charity that looks after cats and dogs which have been found in the street
10. a charity that helps artists who have financial difficulties

2. Work in small groups. Choose a charity that everyone in the group feels comfortable with – or make one up. Design a poster for the charity. Think about:

– what you want people to do
– how to catch their attention
– what images you might want on your poster
– what information you might want to get across
– a slogan/catchphrase
– how people can give money/contact you

Compare your answers with other groups.

Jewellery for men

Discussion

Answer the appropriate questions below.

Now compare your answers in small groups. Try and make sure the groups are not all men or all women.

QUESTIONS FOR MEN

1. Do you wear/have you ever worn jewellery?
2. Make a list of all the jewellery you own.
3. How expensive is/was it?
4. Why do you wear it?
5. Are there other items of jewellery that you would like to own and wear? What?
6. Would you wear any of the following?
   a) more than one ring
   b) an earring
   c) a necklace
   d) a brooch

QUESTIONS FOR WOMEN

1. Do you wear jewellery every day or just on special occasions?
2. Do you know any men who wear jewellery? What do they wear?
3. Do you think that generally men look good in jewellery?
4. Would the type of jewellery a man wears influence your attitude towards him?
5. Which of the following do you think men should not wear?
   a) earrings   c) brooches
   b) necklaces   d) toe-rings

Reading

Read the article below and answer these questions:

1. What type of jewellery does David Beckham wear a lot at the moment?
2. Why does Mona Drewitt think that David Beckham wears this kind of jewellery?
3. How popular are wedding rings amongst British men?

DIAMONDS ARE A BOY'S BEST FRIEND

Did you see David Beckham on a German TV chat show the other night? Really? Did you notice what he was wearing? He looked as if he'd bought half a jeweller's shop on the way to the studio. 'He seems to be just crazy about diamonds these days,' says Mona Drewitt from Hatton Garden, London's street for jewellers. And she's right. £50,000 of diamond-studded watch, diamond-studded crosses on his ears, a diamond-studded ring on his little finger. He probably had most of one £100,000 weekly wage packet dispersed about his body as he stepped into the studio that night.

Of course, wearing your wealth is a tradition among nomadic people; like carrying your money around with you because you don't trust banks. Displaying showy and expensive jewellery tells the rest of the world that you're rich. It's also a secret challenge: 'Are you doing as well as me?' 'I'm sure that David Beckham's taste is a conscious way of displaying his wealth,' says Mona Drewitt.

But does such a display show taste and style or is it just plain naff? Do real men wear jewels and rings? Whilst most British men, even if they could afford it, would not go for Becks' diamond-studded accessories, many wear a ring on their little finger, or a wedding ring, or sometimes, daringly, both. However, John Morgan, author of Debrett's *New Guide to Etiquette and Modern Manners* warns: 'The higher up the social ladder you go, the more resistant people are to male jewellery. I wouldn't recommend it to anyone.' That sounds like a red card and back to the dressing room for Mr David Beckham!

Discussion

Discuss these questions in pairs or small groups:

1. What do you think about the amount of jewellery that young sportsmen and other celebrities wear? Does it show good taste or bad taste?
2. Why do people sometimes 'wear their wealth'?
3. Do you think men should wear jewellery? Why/Why not?
4. What about women? Do you think they can sometimes wear too much jewellery?

Language

Label the pictures with the following words:

locket   *ring*   *necklace*   *brooch*   *tiara*   *bracelet*   *chain*   *earring*

Discuss with a partner which of the items of jewellery above you like on men and which on women. Which styles of the items above do you like?

Discussion

Work in pairs or small groups. Look at the pictures below and discuss these questions:

1. Do you like what the person has done to themselves? Why/Why not?
2. If this person was a friend of yours and they had suddenly changed their appearance to look like this, what would you say to them?
3. How would you feel if one of your children came home looking like this?
4. What would you say to them?
5. Would you ever do this?/Have you ever done this?

Who cares about the environment?

Discussion

Work in pairs or small groups. Make lists of:

1. any animals or birds that are endangered or protected in your country
2. any areas of land which are protected
3. any trees or plants which are protected

What is being done to ensure that these things are protected?

Reading

Read the letter below and answer these questions:

1. Who do you think the letter is written to?
2. Which of the following is the best summary of the writer's view of the environment?
   a. We should do everything we can to protect it.
   b. We really shouldn't worry about it at all.
   c. We should be more thoughtful about what we protect.

Dear Sir

I follow your environmental news section with interest. However, as a result of a number of recent stories, I believe that we have begun to take conservation too seriously.

You report that almost 1,000 trees have been cut down in the north of England to create a nature reserve for a tiny snail. Is this sensible? The snail was last seen seven years ago and nobody has seen one since. For all we know, it might already be extinct and 1,000 trees have been cut down for no reason at all.

The world's smallest lizard, measuring 2 cm from nose to tail, has just been discovered in the Dominican Republic and immediately placed on the list of endangered species. Why? A week ago we didn't even know it existed. Why should we suddenly care so much about it now?

At Worthing, on the south coast of England, work has stopped on a sea wall in order to protect the habitat of a rare flower, which was being disturbed by the building work. How much will the people who live there be disturbed if the sea breaks through the sea wall, damaging property and possibly taking lives?

Yes, the environment is important – but more important is human progress, the lives of other species, and a sense of perspective.

Yours faithfully

Reginald Wells

Reginald Wells

Read the letter again and answer these questions:

1. What three conservation issues does the writer mention?
2. What has been done in each case?
3. How does the writer feel about each issue?

Discussion

Discuss these questions in pairs or small groups:

1. How far do you agree with the writer? Give reasons.
2. Can you think of any important environmental or conservation issues in your local area or your country?
3. Describe them to a partner and explain the arguments on each side.
4. What is your opinion about what is happening in these cases?

Language

Look at the underlined expression with *know* in this sentence:

For all we know, it might already be extinct.

It has the meaning of 'this might be true but we just don't know.'

Read these sentences and complete them with expressions from the box:

> a. *You know as well as I do that ...*
>
> b. *He doesn't know the meaning of the word.*
>
> c. *She's such a know-all.*
>
> d. *you never know ...*
>
> e. *... how was I to know ...*
>
> f. *I don't know about you, but ...*

1. Conservation? Don't talk to Gerald about conservation. . . . .
2. . . . . I really can't see the point of struggling to save species that will probably die out anyway.
3. We have to do something to keep people away from these birds' nests. . . . . someone will try to steal the eggs.
4. I didn't mean to embarrass her, but . . . . she worked for a multinational oil company?
5. I hate discussing important issues with Rachel. . . . .
6. I just refuse to eat hamburgers unless I make them myself. I mean, ... what they put in commercially produced ones.

Discussion

1. Work in small groups. Read and discuss each statement below. If everyone agrees with a statement, leave it as it is. If someone disagrees, change the statement so that everyone in the group agrees with it. Use phrases from the Language activity, if appropriate.

1. Plants and animals have been dying out since the beginning of time. It's natural. And it's pointless trying to stop it happening.
2. Humankind has always exploited the resources of the planet – animal, mineral and vegetable. It is nature's problem – not ours.
3. Few species are worth saving: lions, elephants, giant pandas maybe; two-centimetre-long lizards, definitely not.
4. People shouldn't get so angry about the use of land. We need houses and factories. There are plenty of green open spaces around the world. If you need to be near one that badly, move!

2. Work in small groups. All the items on the list below are threatened with extinction. You have the power to save just three. Which three would you save and why?

the Sicilian fir tree
the giant panda
the Sentani rainbowfish
the Chinese alligator
the Virginia round-leaf birch tree
the bowhead whale
a type of Sri Lankan ant
the red wolf

Compare your decision with other groups.

The power of prayer

Discussion

Have you ever prayed in any of the following situations?

1. when you have been ill?
2. before a meal?
3. when a close friend or relative has been having an operation?
4. before going to sleep at night?
5. when you have been in an aircraft that is taking off or landing?
6. before a sporting event – an important football match or race, perhaps?
7. when you have been rushing because you were late for something?
8. before a meeting?
9. after a success of some kind?

Compare your answers in pairs or small groups.

Reading

Read the three short articles below and choose one of the following reactions for each one. Do you have a different reaction?

a: That's just nonsense! I don't believe it.
b: That's fascinating. I can well believe it's true.
c: That's interesting, but I wonder if there's another explanation.

Compare and discuss your reactions in pairs or small groups.

DEMAND FOR KORAN AND BIBLE
After the terrorist attacks of 11th September, many booksellers throughout the UK reported a significant increase in sales of the Bible, in some cases a rise of as much as 25%. One internet bookseller reported that their Bibles sales had not increased, but that there was more demand for copies of the Koran and books on the prophecies of Nostradamus.*

PRAY AND GET PREGNANT
A scientific study on a group of women undergoing fertility treatment suggests that prayer gives women a greater chance of getting pregnant. In this study, reported in the *Journal of Reproductive Medicine,* women who were prayed for had a 50% chance of becoming pregnant, compared with 26% for women who were not prayed for.

PRAYER SAVES PLANE
There was a lucky escape yesterday for the 157 passengers and crew on board a KiteAir jet flying from the Philippines to Hong Kong. Ash from the volcano, Mount Pinatubo, blocked the air intakes, forcing the engines to stop. The pilot, however, managed to restart them once the plane reached clearer air and landed the plane safely at Manila airport. Soledad Garcia, a passenger on the flight, said: "The engines seemed to be stopped for some time. We all prayed that they would start again. There were Muslims, Hindus, and Christians on the plane. Our Gods must have heard us."

*Nostradamus (1503-1566) was a French physician and mystic, famous for publishing prophecies. He has many followers today. You will find lots of websites devoted to his ideas.

Discussion

Discuss these questions about the articles in pairs or small groups:

1. Are you surprised that sales of the Bible rose after September 11th 2001? Why/Why not?
2. Do you believe that prayer really has the power to increase women's fertility or to help the sick? Or do you think that the research is flawed in some way?
3. Do you think prayer was in any way responsible for the engines restarting on the KiteAir plane?
4. What effect(s) do you think prayer has – on the person praying? And on the object (person or thing) of the prayer?

Language

Look at the expressions below to do with believing and disbelieving. Mark each expression as follows:

B = it expresses belief
D = it expresses lack of belief

1. I don't believe a word of that!
2. I'm sure that's right.
3. I've no trouble with that.
4. I have my doubts about that.
5. That seems unlikely to me.
6. You're kidding.
7. I've always suspected that.
8. I can easily believe that.
9. I've never heard such nonsense.
10. I find that difficult to believe.

Read the following attitudes to prayer. Which of the expressions above best describe your own view? Compare your views with a partner.

- If someone is sick, it will help them if you pray for their recovery.
- Prayer is pointless.
- If more people prayed, the world would be a far better place.
- A lot of people only pray when they're in some sort of trouble.
- Atheists have just as good a life as believers.
- Prayer makes you feel better, but it doesn't actually make any difference.
- Prayer is a natural human response to a serious or dangerous situation.
- I pray 6 times every day.
- Prayer is just a form of meditation – nothing else.
- If a lot of people get comfort from prayer, why knock it?

"Well, really! You'd think by now he'd have picked up English!"

Discussion

With a partner, choose one of the three areas below. Discuss the questions, then report to the rest of the class.

1. Your own beliefs

Would you say that you are religious?
Do you pray? When? How often?
How about your friends and family?
Is there a tradition of religion in your family?
Is religion more important for the older or for the younger members of the family?
A recent survey suggests that 70% of people start to pray when they get into difficulty. Do you pray when you get into difficulty? If so, in what sort of circumstances?

2. Religion in your country

What are the main religions in your country?
How important is religion in your culture?
How important is religion in the history of your country?
What percentage of the population is religious?
Is religion more important or less important than it used to be?

3. Holy places

Are there any places of pilgrimage in your country?
Have you been to any of them? Why?
Do you believe that these places possess special powers?
Do you know anyone who has been cured by visiting one of these places?

Revenge is sweet!

Discussion

Discuss these questions with a partner:

Have you ever been really embarrassed in public?
Was it your fault or did someone else embarrass you? What happened?
How did you feel? What did you do afterwards?

Reading

Read the first paragraph of this newspaper article about a vicar and choose the best headline below:

SCANDAL IN CHURCH
VICAR CHEATS ON LOCAL DOCTOR
DOCTOR ATTACKS CHEATING VICAR

A married vicar has left his job after having an affair with the wife of a local doctor. Dr Mark Lucas, 36, interrupted the Rev David Hughes during a church service to call him 'a liar, a cheat and a shameless adulterer' after finding letters from Rev Hughes to his wife.

"They suspect arson."

Discuss these questions:

1. How do you think Dr Lucas felt?
2. How do you think Rev Hughes felt?
3. What do you think happened next in the church?
4. What do you think happened after the church service?

Read the rest of the article and answer these questions:

5. Did Dr Lucas go to the church so that he could embarrass Rev Hughes?
6. What did the other people in the church do?
7. Where is Dr Lucas' wife now?

Gary Buxton, a retired taxi driver, who was attending the church service, said: 'Everything went very quiet. We were all a bit shocked. Then David walked out of the church and no one has seen him since.' Dr Lucas said: 'I had not intended to make a scene. But when he started preaching to people how to live their lives, I saw red. I have seen my solicitor and am seeking a divorce. I won't share a house with her any longer. Not even for the sake of the children.' The Lucases have three children, aged 12, 10 and 8. Rev Hughes and his wife have a grown-up daughter. Mrs Lucas, a teacher at St Mark's Primary School, is believed to have left the area with Rev Hughes. Mrs Hughes was not available for comment.

Discussion

1. How do you feel about what the different people have done – Dr Lucas, Mrs Lucas, Rev Hughes, Mrs Hughes? Have they behaved well, badly, or just like normal people?
2. What would you have done if you had been in the church?
3. What would you have done if you were the vicar's wife – left him or stood by your man?

Language

1. Complete the text below with the correct form of these verb phrases:

have an affair   *leave*   *get a divorce*   *work out*   *be together*   *split up*

I don't really understand Helen and James at all. They . . . . (1) a couple of years ago when James . . . . (2) with his secretary. But then when that didn't . . . . (3), he moved back in with Helen. Then she . . . . . . (4) him for her tennis coach and at that point I thought they were going to . . . . (5). Now they . . . . (6) again and they seem to be as happy as ever.

2. Complete the sentences below with appropriate forms of the following phrases:

paint the town red   *go red*   *be caught red-handed*   *see red*

1. I'm not surprised he . . . . He was extremely embarrassed.
2. He couldn't pretend he was innocent. He . . . .
3. I couldn't help getting angry. When she accused me of lying, I just . . . .
4. We've really got something to celebrate. Let's . . . .

Discussion

Work in pairs. Discuss the questions below:

1. Are you generally vengeful or forgiving? Give examples.
2. If you were surfing the internet and you found a website like the one below, would you:
   a) add it to your favourites – you know you will need it.
   b) read it – it will help you with a present problem.
   c) move on – it's a stupid site.

VENGEANCE-IS-MINE.COM

Has someone treated you badly? Do you need to get your own back?

At vengeance-is-mine.com we are all too aware that some people are greatly in need of humiliation – the pompous, the contemptuous, the violent, the thoughtless. They will all benefit from a little anonymous payback. We do not encourage anything illegal, violent, or in any way damaging. We do not take responsibility for the actions of people who visit this site. We do encourage the victims of revenge to rethink their behaviour. We do hope that the ideas you may find here will be useful.

1. ideas for revenge
2. classic revenge stories
3. things to buy
4. help our members

---

3. Can you imagine ever using anything on the list below to get revenge on someone? What might you use the items for?

a box of melted chocolates   *an old love letter from a friend's ex-boyfriend*
itching powder   *a photograph of a friend as a fat 5-year-old child*
a bunch of artificial black roses   *an empty box for flowers*
a miniature tombstone   *a subscription form for a rude magazine*

4. With a partner, decide what you would do in the following situations:
   a. Your partner (boy/girlfriend or spouse) has run off with your best friend.
   b. A friend borrowed £200 from you last year and has never paid you back. She is avoiding you.
   c. You bought a car from someone you know and it keeps breaking down.
   d. A friend borrowed a CD from you two years ago and has never returned it.
   e. Your boss keeps giving you really boring, unpleasant jobs to do.
   f. A colleague at work keeps telling everyone how wonderful he is.

A matter of birth and death

Discussion

1. Do you know any couples who are childless?
2. Do you think that more couples are childless because they don't want children or because they can't have children?
3. Do you know any couples who have had IVF (in vitro fertilisation) treatment? Was it successful?

Reading

Read the article below. Mark these sentences T (true) or F (false):

1. Diane Blood died after a fight.
2. Stephen Blood is Liam's father.
3. Diane Blood was treated in Britain.

> **SECOND CHILD FOR DIANE**
>
> Diane Blood, the widow who spent two years fighting the courts for the right to have a child using her late husband's sperm, is now pregnant with a second child also from his sperm.
>
> Diane's husband, Stephen Blood, became ill with meningitis in March 1995, aged 30. The couple had been trying to start a family. While Stephen lay dying in hospital, Diane persuaded doctors to remove and freeze a sample of his sperm. The Human Fertilisation and Embryo
>
> Authority initially refused to allow Diane Blood to use the sperm because her husband had not given permission in writing. However, the appeal court later decided that she could take the sperm abroad for treatment under EU law. Her son, Liam, was born three and a half years after his father's death.
>
> Diane Blood said: 'I'm an only child but Stephen had two sisters. He would have been delighted that Liam is to be raised with a full brother or sister, and that he is to be a father again.'

Discussion

1. With a partner, try to agree on one alternative from each of the following:

1. a. It was right that Stephen Blood's sperm was removed. He would have agreed.
   b. It was wrong that the sperm was removed without Stephen's consent.

2. a. It was a disgrace that she could not be treated in Britain.
   b. Britain is right to have such strict laws about this kind of thing.

3. a. Diane should not have been allowed to do this a second time.
   b. It is crazy that governments should become involved. This is a matter for the individual.

4. a. It is wrong to bring children into the world with no father present.
   b. A single mother can be just as good a parent.

2. How do you think the parents of Stephen Blood felt at the birth of the first child? Do you think they are happy at the idea of another grandchild?

3. What is the situation in your country?

a. The law is very strict and it is very difficult to do something like this.
b. The law is very progressive and Diane Blood would have had no trouble doing what she did.
c. My country has no official policy on things like this.

4. Are you aware of any cases like Diane Blood's in your country?

Language

Complete the text using the correct forms of the appropriate verbs from the box below:

expect	*give*	*adopt*
marry	*start*	*fall*
be	*raise*	*lose*

Jason and Annie . . . . (1) in March 1990. Very soon afterwards they decided to . . . . (2) a family and Annie became pregnant very quickly. Their first child, a son, ... (3) born at the beginning of 1991. Annie loved children and six months later she . . . . (4) another baby. In spring 1992 Annie . . . . (5) birth to a baby girl. Tragically, however, there were complications at the birth and Annie died a few days later. Jason gave up his job and . . . . (6) the children on his own for five years. Then he met Lucy, ... (7) in love with her and they got married. Lucy loved Jason's children but really wanted some of her own. After . . . . (8) two babies in early pregnancy, the doctors told her that she was unlikely ever to be able to have children of her own. As a result, Jason and Lucy decided to . . . . (9) a baby, which they did in 1999. Jason's son and daughter think their new baby sister is wonderful.

Discussion

1. IVF

Which of the options below do you think are acceptable courses of action for a couple who are unable to have children?

- IVF treatment in which the mother's egg is fertilised with the sperm of her husband or partner
- IVF treatment using the mother's egg and sperm from a sperm bank
- paying another woman to have a baby using your husband's sperm

2. Adoption

What kind of people should be allowed to adopt children? Here are six different situations. Do you think any of these people should be stopped from adopting?

1. a young man and woman in their mid-twenties who have been married for three years and cannot have children
2. a lesbian couple in their thirties who want a child
3. a couple in their mid-forties who have just got married
4. a couple in their late thirties who have been married for twelve years and cannot have children
5. a couple of gay men in their thirties who want to bring up a child
6. a couple in their early fifties who have grown-up children by their first marriages, but want to start a second family now that they have re-married

3. Many people adopt children from abroad. Which of the following is closest to your view?

1. It is better for children to grow up in a loving family in the West than in an orphanage in their own country.
2. It is immoral to remove children from their own country and culture.
3. No child should be adopted by people from another country without the consent of the child's natural parents.
4. This is a very difficult issue and it depends on the situation of the children and their natural parents.

Finally

Diane Blood gave birth to her second child, another boy, Joel Michael, seven years after the removal of her dying husband's sperm. All four grandparents were present. The baby was born in Britain, but Mrs Blood had had to go to Belgium to be inseminated. One particular disappointment for Diane was the refusal of the British authorities to allow her to put her husband's name on her children's birth certificates. There are thought to be about 40 women in Britain in a similar situation to Diane Blood.

If you look on the internet, you will find more about the ethics of cases like this.

Folk wisdom

Introduction

Read these two sayings and discuss the questions below in pairs or small groups:

Give a man a fish and you feed him for a day; teach him how to fish and you feed him for a lifetime.
Red sky at night, shepherd's delight; red sky in the morning, shepherd's warning.

1. What do the sayings mean?
2. Do you think they are useful?
3. What part of the world do you think they come from?
4. Do you have any similar sayings in your language?

Reading

Read the text below and answer these questions:

1. What do we know about Murphy?
2. What is the basic idea behind all of Murphy's laws?

MURPHY'S LAWS

It was a man called Murphy, about whom we seem to know nothing other than his name and his pessimistic view of life, who first made the profound revelation that if anything can go wrong, it will. This simple idea about the way the world works has since planted itself in the human mind with a deep and lasting effect on the way we live. From his first and most famous law – 'If anything can go wrong, it will' – Murphy went on to develop his theories, creating other related principles that govern our lives. Undoubtedly one of the most important thinkers of our time, Murphy has seen to the very heart of our existence and opened our eyes to the mysterious ways of fate. Murphy's inspiration is often seen as a defining moment in global history, copied by many, but equalled by none.

- If anything can go wrong, it will.
- If there is a possibility of several things going wrong, the one that will cause the most damage will be the one to go wrong. Note: If there is a worse time for something to go wrong, it will happen then.
- If anything just cannot go wrong, it will anyway.
- If you see that there are four possible ways in which something can go wrong, and take precautions against these, then a fifth way, which you have not prepared for, will suddenly develop.
- Left to themselves, things tend to go from bad to worse.
- If everything seems to be going well, you have obviously overlooked something.

A further important rule to remember is:
- A knowledge of Murphy's Law is no help in any situation.

Discussion

Work in pairs or small groups. Discuss these questions:

1. How important does the writer say that Murphy's theories are?
2. How serious is the writer?
3. Can you think of any examples of Murphy's Law applying in your life or the lives of people you know?
4. Do you have similar 'laws' in your country?

Language

Sayings, proverbs and 'laws' are often told using a form of conditional sentence. For example:

If anything can go wrong, it will.

Add to the list of sayings below with ideas from your country/culture:

1. If you tell a dream before breakfast, it will come true.
2. If you walk under a ladder, you will have bad luck.
3. If your nose itches, somebody is coming to visit.
4. . . . .
5. . . . .
6. . . . .
7. . . . .
8. . . . .

Compare your sentences in pairs or small groups.

Discussion

1. Work in pairs. Complete the sayings below with words from the box:

have	*postpone*	*grow*	*show*
see	*consists*	*is*	*has*

1. Children . . . . . . more need of models than of critics.
2. Don't let grass . . . . . . on the path of friendship.
3. Doubt . . . . . . the key to knowledge.
4. People . . . . . . their character by what they laugh at.
5. Heroism . . . . . . of hanging on one minute longer.
6. You can't . . . . . . the whole sky through a bamboo tube.
7. Liberty . . . . . . no price.
8. . . . . . . today's anger until tomorrow.

What is the point of each saying?
Have you heard any of them before?

2. Where do you think each saying comes from? Match each of the above with the following sources:

Germany	*the Philippines*
Norway	*Spain*
Japan	*France*
Iran	*Native American*

Discussion

1. Sometimes people claim that there are rational, or even historical, explanations for a lot of our folk wisdom. For example:

The idea that it is lucky to put a horseshoe over our front door comes from a time when it was believed that witches rode on broomsticks because they were afraid of horses. Putting a horseshoe over your door kept witches away.

The idea of having seven years' bad luck if you break a mirror comes from the time when mirrors were very expensive. If you broke yours, it would take seven years to save the money for a new one.

2. Can you think of any rational or historical explanations for these sayings?

1. The tail of a fox dead of old age brings good luck.
2. Never touch a baby, a mother and a tombstone all in one day.
3. Nothing succeeds like success.
4. Never argue at a crossroads.

3. What about for these actions?

1. Touching wood.
2. Making the sign of the cross.
3. Putting a tooth that has come out under your pillow at night.
4. Making a wish when you cut your birthday cake.
5. Shaking hands with your right hand (not your left).

Some more sayings

Here are some more sayings. Do you think there is any truth in any of them? Are they amusing, insightful or just stupid? Do you have similar sayings in your country? What are they?

The light at the end of the tunnel is a train.
Those who know the least will always know it loudest.
Beauty is only skin deep, fashion is even shallower.
An expert is someone with an opinion and a word processor.
Everything tastes more or less like chicken.
There are three kinds of memory: good, bad and convenient.

I'm on the train!

Discussion

Work in pairs or small groups. Discuss these questions:

1. Do you have a mobile phone? If not, why not?
2. How many people do you know who don't have a mobile phone?
3. If you have a mobile phone, do you use it for both calls and texting? How often?
4. What is the most embarrassing situation in which your mobile phone has rung?
5. What is the most embarrassing situation in which someone else's mobile phone has rung?
6. What is the most irritating ring tone you have heard?
7. What is the most amusing ring tone you have heard?

"Hello – yeah – I'm on the train."

Reading

Read the article and tick (✔) the correct sentence below:

The writer thinks: a. too many people have mobile phones.
                     b. mobile phones are fantastic.
                     c. people worry about how to behave with a mobile phone.

FULLY MOBILE

True stories or urban myths? Everyone has tales about mobiles – but they always happen to someone else.

Have you heard the one about the pregnant woman on the train? She was sitting opposite some bloke, who was talking noisily and at length into his mobile. She started to go into labour and asked to borrow his phone to call her doctor. He refused. Why? Well, positively writhing with embarrassment, he was forced to admit his phone wasn't real.

Or how about the boxer in a restaurant loudly negotiating the terms of his next fight into a phone which suddenly rang? Or the Italian priest who interrupted a religious ceremony to take a call?

Everyone has a story, but almost everyone has a mobile too. Mobile ownership is now well over 50% in the UK, and heading ever closer to Finland where a remarkable 75% of the population own a mobile.

Are we put off by potential health risks? No. What about the possibility of being mugged for our phone? It won't happen to me. Or how about the thought that we might look a complete idiot on the 6.15 from Paddington saying 'I'm on the train'. Good heavens, no! Not me! For me they're an endless source of amusement and fascination. In fact, I'm in mobile heaven.

Discussion

Work in pairs. Discuss these questions:

1. What risks or dangers are mentioned in the article? Can you think of any other risks or dangers not mentioned?
2. Do you think the stories in the article are true or not? Do you know of any similar stories?

Language 1

Study this sentence:

(She was) sitting opposite some bloke, who was talking noisily and at length into his mobile.

'Bloke' is a slang word meaning 'man'. Slang is a kind of colloquial language which can make speech more vivid and interesting. However, you must be careful not to use it in inappropriate situations. Match the underlined slang word in the sentences 1-8 to the definitions in the box below:

1. You couldn't lend me some money, could you? I'm <u>skint.</u>
2. Let's go somewhere else for a drink. I've just seen the <u>cops</u> go in there.
3. And then she dropped her glass and spilt red wine on their new carpet. She's such a <u>plonker.</u>
4. Just a minute! I must go to the <u>loo</u> before we go.
5. I'll bring some food if you could bring the <u>booze.</u>
6. I think he was a bit <u>pissed.</u> He couldn't walk straight and he laughed too loudly.
7. You should ask that <u>guy</u> over there – the one with the green hat.
8. Joe's down at the police station. He <u>nicked</u> some CDs in the new shopping centre and got caught.

a. stupid person	e. stole
b. drunk	f. alcohol
c. having no money	g. lavatory
d. police	h. man

Language 2

Complete the text below with appropriate forms of the slang words from the exercise above:

I got on the train home the other day and this . . . . (1) with red hair got on and sat down opposite me. I knew he was a . . . . (2) as soon as he got out his mobile. He rang his girlfriend and started talking to her. The whole carriage could hear what he was saying. After a while I realised he was . . . . (3) as well. I could smell the . . . . (4) on his breath and there was a bottle of whisky sticking out of his pocket. Anyway, the next thing I know a couple of . . . . (5) got on the train and came up to him. They asked him where he got the whisky. He looked a bit embarrassed. So they arrested him because they reckoned he . . . . (6) it from a shop just outside the station and they'd got him on the security cameras.

"Spare the price of a cup of tea?"

Discussion

1. Read this short article and discuss the questions below in pairs or small groups:

> A 'stubborn and arrogant' airline passenger was jailed for a year yesterday after refusing to switch off his mobile phone on an international flight. Judge Anthony Ensor told the shocked oil worker, Neil Whitehouse, that the sentence was intended to discourage other people who might be tempted to behave in a similar fashion.

1. Does the article surprise you?
2. Does the punishment surprise you?
3. Do you think the punishment is too strict or not strict enough? Why?

2. You have been asked to draw up a list of rules for people using mobile phones in public. Work in pairs or small groups. Think about the following:

1. when and where it is appropriate to use them
2. when and where it is not appropriate
3. the length of calls
4. the type of conversations allowed
5. ringtones
6. possible punishments for breaking the rules

Children and discipline

Discussion

Work in pairs. Make a list of ways in which parents and teachers discipline children. For each punishment on the list discuss the following questions:

1. Is this a reasonable punishment to give a child in a civilised society?
2. What age of child is it suitable for?
3. Who can give this punishment to a child? Parents? Teachers? Other relatives?

Reading

Read these two letters. Which one do you agree most with? Why?

Dear Sir

I think it is quite ridiculous that the government should be considering legislation to ban smacking. Every parent needs the right to be able to give a child a smack, not in order to cause physical harm or pain, but more as a shock tactic to stop a child from misbehaving or in some circumstances to stop them causing damage to themselves or other people. Some people argue that laws are needed to stop excessive physical punishment, but there are quite clear laws dealing with assault and bodily harm. If a parent causes physical harm to a child, then the police can use these laws to bring the parent to justice. My father used to give me the slipper and it never did me any harm. What is all the fuss about?

Jack Wallace

Dear Sir

Thank goodness the government has finally begun to see sense regarding the punishment of children! Let us hope that they have the courage to do away with the physical punishment of children. We supposedly live in a civilised society. Can we at last realise that physical punishment is unreasonable, degrading, mentally harmful and completely unacceptable in the 21st century? Smacking, indeed any form of physical punishment, should be made illegal immediately, and parents and teachers who practise this disgraceful activity should be brought before the courts.

Laura Flynn

Make four true sentences:

Jack Wallace Laura Flynn	would like to see all physical punishment banned. thinks the laws are acceptable as they are now. thinks smacking has more than a physical effect. was smacked as a child.

Discussion

Work in small groups. Discuss these statements:

'An adult hitting a child of any age is not right and there are much better ways to discipline children.'

'Children should have the same rights as adults. Adults cannot hit other adults, so they should not be allowed to hit children either.'

Do you agree or not? Why?

Are there other, better ways of disciplining children?

Language

Study this sentence from the second letter. Notice the phrasal verb with two particles 'to do away with' meaning *to abolish*.

Let us hope that they have the courage to <u>do away with</u> the physical punishment of children.

Match the phrasal verbs underlined in the sentences 1-8 with the definitions a-h below:

1. My brother was always in trouble but he was too honest. If I was in trouble I always denied doing anything wrong and I usually <u>got away with</u> it!
2. When I <u>look back on</u> my childhood, I realise my parents treated me really very fairly.
3. If I <u>ran out of</u> money, I would sometimes 'borrow' some from my mother's purse.
4. Sometimes I wished my dad would just give me a smack. It would have been better than listening to him <u>going on about</u> 'responsibility'.
5. I can remember the first time I <u>stood up to</u> my dad. He wanted to punish me for coming back after midnight when I was 15 but I just told him I wasn't a child any longer and he couldn't tell me what to do.
6. I don't exactly <u>look down on</u> parents who smack their children, but I do think that they could find other ways of disciplining their children if they really thought about it.
7. I was really badly behaved when I was a teenager but I seemed to <u>grow out of</u> it when I reached my early twenties.
8. I didn't get into much trouble at school – except for once when I was caught <u>fooling around with</u> some chemicals in a science laboratory.

a. *to not run away from, to resist*
b. *to escape without punishment*
c. *to consider inferior*
d. *to think about something in the past*
e. *to become too old to do something*
f. *to not have any left*
g. *to behave irresponsibly*
h. *to talk about something for a long time and in a boring way*

Work in pairs. Look at the sentences again. Are any of them true for you?

Do any of them remind you of people you know or knew?

"Frankly, I feel he over-disciplines his animals."

Discussion

Work in pairs or small groups. Discuss these questions:

1. Which, if any, of the punishments below do you think are unsuitable for children above the age of three?

   a. a quick smack on the hand
   b. a quick smack on the back of the head
   c. a smack on the bottom
   d. a smack on the bare bottom
   e. a blow from a slipper on the bare bottom
   f. a blow from a belt on the hand
   g. a blow from a cane on the bottom

Would it make any difference if the child was a boy or a girl?
What other factors might determine whether a particular punishment was reasonable or not?

2. Which, if any, of these punishments do you think is acceptable?

   a. sending a child to their bedroom for an hour
   b. not allowing the child to play with their friends for a week
   c. stopping the child's pocket money
   d. not allowing the child to watch TV for a week
   e. making the child stay behind at school to do extra work
   f. giving the child extra jobs around the house

3. At what age do you think it is no longer necessary or appropriate to discipline children?

Ever eaten dog?

Introduction

Mark the items listed below as follows:

0 = I have never eaten it.
1 = I have eaten it once or twice.

2 = I eat it quite often.
3 = I eat it a lot.

steak	fish	horse	ostrich	bacon	chicken/egg
dog	eel or snake	shellfish	deer	goose	insects

Compare your answers in pairs or small groups.

Reading

Read the article below and then answer these questions:

1. What did the writer do?
2. Why did he do it?
3. How did he feel about it?

> **CANINE CUISINE**
>
> Guess what? I've eaten dog. And not only did I eat it, I ate it because I wanted to. I ate three courses of it. I enjoyed it. And I don't care what you think. I was in Seoul, South Korea, sent there to write some background articles before the start of the 2002 World Cup. International pressure on the Koreans to stop eating dog was not having any discernable effect. The Koreans were upset, understandably, at the hypocritical attitude of 'snail-eating, horsemeat-eating Westerners'. How, as an impartial journalist, could I write an informed piece on dog-eating? Obviously I had to try some.
>
> My taxi driver nearly had an accident when I asked him to take me to the best dog restaurant in town. Westerners don't do that. The head waiter looked surprised too, but politely explained the menu to me.
>
> You may not believe this, but at home I am largely vegetarian – though more from fear of 'scientific' farming methods than from ethics. So partly because of that, and partly because of memories of much-loved childhood pets, I braced myself with a couple of beers before the food arrived.
>
> I started slowly. But then, with increasing enthusiasm, I tucked into my starter of poshintang, a wonderful doggy soup; followed by soo yuck, dog slices; and then jin-guk, dog casserole. Yum!
>
> Neighbouring diners watched with interest as this Westerner appreciated their fine Korean delicacies! Whilst not a sight they will ever see again – too strong are my vegetarian sentiments – I must stress it was not an experience about which I feel any guilt.

True or false?

Read the article again. Mark the following sentences T (true) or F (false):

1. The writer had been sent to research some articles on Korean cuisine.
2. Koreans rarely see Westerners eating dog.
3. The writer eats a lot of meat at home.
4. The writer liked dog so much he plans to make it a regular part of his diet.

Discussion

Work in pairs or small groups and discuss the following questions:

1. Do you think the writer needed to eat dog to be able to write an article?
2. If you had been in the writer's position, would you have eaten dog?
3. Would you ever eat dog? Why/Why not?
4. Are there things which people in your country eat that people from other countries find unpleasant?
5. Is eating dog any worse than eating lamb or veal? Why/Why not?

Language

Describing food

1. Put these adjectives into the appropriate group below:

fatty	tough	delicious	appetising
tasty	sweet	bitter	disgusting
rich	spicy	inedible	mouth-watering
sour	bland	oily	tasteless

a. to describe the general quality of food

. . . .

. . . .

b. to describe a particular quality of food

. . . .

. . . .

2. In the box above, mark each adjective:

- **+ = positive**
- **− = negative**

3. Choose a negative adjective from the box to describe each of these foods:

a. steak   . . . .
b. salad dressing . . . .
c. coffee   . . . .
d. curry   . . . .
e. lemon   . . . .

4. Think of other types of food which can be described by the above adjectives. For example:

Oranges can be bitter.
Frogs' legs probably taste disgusting.

Discussion

1. Work in pairs or small groups. Discuss these questions in pairs or small groups:

1. What is the most unusual thing you have ever eaten?
2. What is the most unusual thing you have ever been offered?
3. Are there any common sorts of food that you really hate? What are they? Why do you hate them?

2. Where do you think the following things are eaten? Match the country or region to the food:

South Africa	*Burma*
Colombia	*Japan*
Cambodia	*California*

1. deep fried tarantula
2. chocolate-dipped scorpion
3. grasshopper marinated in soy sauce
4. deep fried ants
5. cockroach kebab
6. termites fried in tomato

Have you ever eaten insects? If so, what sort? What did they taste like? If not, what do you think they taste like?

3. Read these articles and discuss the questions:

> Sepp Blatter, President of FIFA, has written to the South Korean Football Association urging them to be sensitive to foreign feelings and to take dog off the menu during the World Cup.

1. Is it acceptable for Sepp Blatter to try and stop the Koreans eating dog? Why/Why not?
2. Does a sports organisation have any right to try and interfere in the eating habits of a nation?

> Brigitte Bardot, French actress and animal rights activist, has outraged the Koreans by using the World Cup to lead a campaign against the eating of dog.

1. Does Brigitte Bardot have any more right than Sepp Blatter to take this attitude? Why/Why not?
2. A Korean politician has said: 'Foreign criticism of dog meat reflects lack of understanding of our nation's ancient culture.' Do you agree? Why/ Why not?

Why not have a look at the following website?
  www.tomatoesareevil.com
Is there one which you would like to set up?

A healthy lifestyle

Discussion

Put a tick (✔) by the things that you think are good for your health and a cross (x) by the things you think are bad for your health.

eating meat	yoga	crisps	smoking	sugar	watching TV
living alone	tea	alcohol	running	coffee	vitamin pills
keeping a pet	salt	flying	sunbathing	stress	being vegetarian

Compare your results in pairs or small groups.

Reading

Read the two letters and answer these questions:

Which writer a) follows the doctor's advice?
              b) thinks the doctor could give better advice?

Dear Doctor

I read your newspaper column every week and, frankly, I think you've got it wrong. It's not being healthy that makes us happy, it's the other way round.
If someone is happy and enjoying themselves and taking pleasure out of life, then they are going to be healthy. Recent research shows that people who feel little or no guilt about their lifestyle have less heart trouble, go to the doctor less often, and get ill less often. In other words, it's not so much <u>what</u> we do as how we feel about it.
As a result, I think you should stop telling people what is bad for them, what they shouldn't eat and where they're going wrong with their lives. You should be encouraging people to feel good about themselves, be positive, worry less and do what they want.

Andrew C, (Newcastle)

Dear Doctor

I always find your column very interesting. Over the years you have given me very useful advice about how to live a healthy life.
However, sometimes I wonder how many people follow your advice. There must be a lot of people who smoke and drink too much, who eat too much sugar and salt and fat, and who generally have a very unhealthy lifestyle.
Surely the government can do something about these people. They are costing our health service huge amounts of money. If they looked after themselves properly, they wouldn't need medical treatment so often.

Angela M, (Brighton)

True or false?

Mark these sentences T (true) or F (false):

1. Andrew thinks health and happiness are not connected.
2. He has done some research into the effect of happiness on health.
3. He thinks the doctor should try to make people happier rather than healthier.
4. Angela thinks a lot of people ignore the doctor's advice.
5. She thinks the health service spends a lot of money on these people.
6. She thinks the government should let them look after themselves rather than provide a health service for them.

Discussion

Discuss these questions in pairs or small groups:

1. Who do you agree with most: Andrew or Angela? Both of them? Neither of them?
2. What are the most important points that they make?
3. To what extent do you 'look after yourself properly'?
4. Do you eat the right food? Smoke? Drink? Take regular exercise?
5. Do you consider yourself to be healthy?
6. Do you consider yourself to be happy?
7. Do you agree with Andrew that there is a connection between health and happiness?

Language

In 1, 2, and 3 there is one word which does not collocate well. Cross it out. Then use expressions from the box to fill the gaps in the sentences below:

> 1. Her health is   perfect.
>   excellent.
>   delicate.
>   major.
>   poor.
>
> 2. She is   disgustingly
>   partially
>   reasonably   healthy.
>   extremely
>   perfectly
>
> 3. It's a healthy   environment.
>   climate.
>   bread.
>   diet.
>   lifestyle.

"Actually, madam, I can recommend everything."

4. I'm afraid my grandmother is in very . . . . She's almost 90.
5. The dry climate of Switzerland makes it a very . . . .
6. What a great tan! You're looking . . . . ! Where've you been?
7. If you don't mind me saying, what you need is a . . . . – things like brown bread, fresh fruit, muesli, that kind of thing.
8. My father's 75. He's got a few health problems, but nothing very serious. His health is . . . . for a man of his age.

Discussion

With a partner, make up a questionnaire to find out how healthy people are.

1. First decide six questions.
2. Think of three different answers for each question.
3. Give marks for each answer.
4. Decide what total of marks mean that people are healthy or unhealthy.
5. Write some praise and/or advice for people based on their marks total.
6. Interview one or two people and note their answers.
7. Tell them how healthy you think they are.

When writing questions you might want to think about some of these areas:

people's diet – the kind of thing they eat
the amount of exercise they take
the amount of stress in their lives
whether they consider they are happy

their lifestyle – busy or laid-back
their own health over the past few years
their past family health history
whether they drink or smoke

Public figures, private lives

Discussion

Discuss these questions in pairs or small groups:

1. Are there any public figures in your country whose private lives are often featured in the press?
2. Who are they? Politicians? Film stars? Pop stars? Sportspeople? Who else?
3. Are any of them only 'famous for being famous'?
4. What aspects of their private lives are reported in the press?
5. Do any of these people object to what is said about them? Why?

Reading

Read the newspaper article. Mark these sentences T (true) or F (false):

1. Natasha Davies was on a Caribbean island.
2. Tom Farrell was on a Caribbean island.
3. Tom Farrell has never met Natasha Davies.
4. The newspapers did not admit their mistake.

IT WASN'T ME!

A deserted, sunsoaked Caribbean beach. A young couple lie sunbathing. They chat. They kiss. They cuddle. They are doing what any young lovers would be doing.

A speed boat a mile off shore. A pair of ugly old journalists with long lenses on their cameras. They do what ugly old journalists do. Three days later the story breaks: city lawyer, Tom Farrell, and Australian soap star, Natasha Davies, photographed on the beach. The photos make the Saturday tabloids and are repeated in some of the Sundays.

By lunchtime on Monday libel writs have hit the desks of half a dozen national newspaper editors. Sure, Farrell has been linked romantically with Davies in the past. But on this occasion, the papers have it completely wrong. It wasn't him on the beach with Davies. And they have the photos to prove it! Despite swift apologies from all the papers concerned, Farrell is seeking damages for 'embarrassment' and the 'negative effect on his personal and professional reputation'. However, Farrell has had well-documented relationships with a number of actresses and pop stars. And he is not usually unhappy about seeing his name in the papers. With such a high-profile lifestyle, it will be interesting to see how much, if anything, he gets from the courts. But far more importantly, if it wasn't him with Natasha Davies, then who was it?

"Surprise!"

Discussion

Discuss these questions in pairs or small groups:

1. What seems to be the writer's attitude towards the journalists who took the photos?
2. Do you approve of what they did or not? Why?
3. Why does the writer think that Tom Farrell will not get very much money from the courts?
4. Do you think this is fair or not? Why?
5. In general, what does the writer's attitude seem to be towards gossip about the private lives of famous people?
6. Do you agree with this attitude or not? Why?

Language

Cross out the collocation in each group which is not natural:

| 1. a(n) casual
      partial
      intimate   relationship
      sexual
      business | 3. a fine
    growing
    well-earned   reputation
    poor
    broad |
| 2. have
    establish
    open   a relationship with …
    break off
    maintain | 4. have
    destroy
    damage   a reputation
    establish
    abolish |

Complete the sentences below with complete expressions from the boxes above:

1. We just have a . . . . We never see each other socially.
2. The stories in the press about his behaviour have completely . . . .
3. She only started her company last year, but she has . . . . for high quality work.
4. They were together for five years before she . . . .
5. Don't buy one of those cars! They have a very . . . . for reliability.
6. After years of hard work, he has finally . . . . as the best lawyer in town.
7. We always try to . . . . good . . . . with our customers.
8. For years I thought we just had a fairly . . . . and then suddenly she asked me to marry her!

Discussion

Use the three questions below to discuss the situations in pairs or small groups:

1. Can the story/photos be in any way considered to be 'in the public interest'?
2. Should the press be allowed to publish the story/photos? Why/why not?
3. If the case goes to court, what should happen?

A famous pop star sells the exclusive pictures of his wedding to a well-known magazine. One of the wedding guests takes some private photos and then sells them to a rival magazine.	Journalists discover that a member of the national football team has ongoing relationships with three women other than his wife.
A pop singer is photographed coming out of a clinic which specialises in plastic surgery.	Journalists discover that a leading politician has been consistently unfaithful to his wife and is currently having an affair with a well-known actress.
A famous TV personality, but one who is rarely mentioned in gossip columns, is photographed sunbathing topless on a private beach while on a holiday with her family.	Journalists discover that a disc jockey on national radio was under the influence of alcohol when recording a programme recently where the audience were all children.

Where do you stand?

The famous argue:

Everyone has 'the right to respect for his private and family life, his home and correspondence.'
(Article 8 – European Human Rights Act)

The press argue:

Everyone has 'the right to freedom of expression, freedom to hold opinions and to receive and impart information and ideas without interference by public authority.'
(Article 10 – European Human Rights Act)

Who is right? Discuss the question in small groups.

Holidays from hell!

Discussion

Work in pairs. Tell each other about the worst holiday you have ever had. Tell each other:

1. what went wrong and why
2. what you did about it
3. how you felt at the time
4. how things turned out in the end

With a different partner, decide if you should get compensation for the following complaints. Then decide the amount you should get.

• One of my fellow guests killed two mice which had come into the hotel dining room from the garden.

• The railings on the balcony blocked the view of the sea when we lay in our deckchairs.

• While on holiday in India, I caught a cold when the air-conditioning in the coach was switched off and the windows opened.

• I found an army of ants marching up the side of my bed.

• I found an insect in my soup. After that, I couldn't eat in the hotel restaurant.

• Even though passengers changed places every day on our 14-day coach tour, I never got to sit in the front seat.

• I saw a cockroach on a plate of cold meat on the buffet.

• Because I was travelling on my own, I had to share a room with another man. He did not smell very nice. He snored, and during the day he behaved strangely.

• I switched on the light in the middle of the night and found 10 cockroaches on the floor beside my bed. I've got a photo to prove it!

Reading

Read the text and find out if you were right.

GERMAN HOLIDAY PROBLEMS

We have discovered a new sport in Germany, or maybe it's a new business: we try and sue our holiday company in the hope of getting back some of the money we paid for the holiday. But when you look at what some people complain about, you do begin to wonder why they went on holiday in the first place.

Unsuccessful claims came from the couple who were upset because the railings on their balcony blocked the seaview when they lay on their deckchairs. Also from the Berlin man who never got to sit in the front seat on his coach tour. Poor chap!

The man who caught a cold because the air-conditioning on the coach was switched off and the windows opened received a similar lack of sympathy.

Insects are a better bet, but by no means foolproof. The woman who woke up to find 10 cockroaches on the floor by her bed got a 50% refund; and the man who discovered 'an army of ants' climbing the side of his bed got 25% back. However, one cockroach on the cold buffet or an insect in a bowl of soup is apparently not enough to spoil a holiday. According to the judge 'you can remove the insect and carry on as normal.'

Mice are no good at all. They naturally live all over the place, so if they find their way from the garden into the dining room, it's not really anybody's fault.

Nor are travelling companions a source of refunds. The man who ended up sharing a room with someone who smelt bad, snored and 'behaved strangely during the day' had his claim refused.

While some of these claims are laughable, some do demand attention. And some of the stranger ones even deserve sympathy – like the cruise passengers whose entertainment turned out to be that 'famous' Briton, Charles Winterton, a 'master' of the five-stringed guitar and of imitating animal noises! So, next time you go on holiday, it may turn out to be cheaper than you think!

Discussion

Discuss the following questions in pairs or small groups:

1. Were you surprised by any of the courts' decisions? Which? Why?
2. Which (if any) of the claims do you feel were completely unreasonable?
3. Which of the situations would you have complained about?
4. Have you ever complained to a holiday company/travel operator? What about? What happened?

Language

Complete these expressions from the text above. Check that you understand what they mean – use a dictionary if necessary.

1. in . . . . hope of   2. in the . . . . place   3. to . . . . a cold   4. a . . . . of sympathy
5. by . . . . means   6. to . . . . a holiday   7. all . . . . the place   8. to deserve . . . .

Complete this text using appropriate forms of the expressions above:

> *Dear Jill*
>
> *Just got back from a week in Devon. It was . . . . (1) the worst holiday I've had, but it certainly wasn't the best. We went there . . . . (2) getting a bit of sunshine and relaxation! Well, the weather was OK, but Dennis certainly knows how . . . . (3). Of course he wouldn't book in advance, so we had to drive . . . . (4) trying to find somewhere to stay. As it was July, most places were full. We eventually found a very nice guest house, but then he managed . . . . (5). He's awful when he's ill but I really didn't think he . . . . . . any . . . . . . (6). So he spent the week complaining about how he was feeling and I had to listen to him. When we got back, we had a terrible argument. He complained that I had shown a complete . . . . (7) for his condition. So I told him I had never wanted to go to Devon . . . . (8). Fortunately, I think we're friends again now! Hope to see you at the barbecue on Friday.*
>
> *Love*
>
> *Amy*

Discussion

1. Quickly make a note of your answer to each of the following questions. Then compare notes in small groups.

1. What's the worst hotel you have ever stayed in?
2. What's the worst flight/boat trip/car journey you have ever made?
3. What's the worst beach you have ever been on?
4. What's the worst thing you have ever eaten on holiday?
5. What's the longest delay you have ever had while travelling?
6. What's the worst holiday illness you have ever had?

2. Work in pairs or small groups. Discuss each of the following quotations. What do you think they mean? Do you agree or disagree with them? Why?

Travel broadens the mind.
To travel hopefully is a better thing than to arrive.
He travels the fastest who travels alone.
Travelling is the ruin of all happiness.
There's no looking at a building here after seeing Italy.
I travel not to go anywhere, but to go. I travel for travel's sake.

"Well, one of us had to go and find the Tourist Information Centre."

The dating game

Discussion

Answer these questions truthfully. Then compare your answers in pairs or small groups.

1. Do you ever read 'Lonely Hearts' ads in the newspaper?
2. Do you ever look at 'Lonely Hearts' websites?
3. Have you ever placed a 'Lonely Hearts' ad in a paper or anywhere else? If so, what happened? Who replied? How did you follow it up? Was it a successful experience? If not, do you think you ever would? Why/Why not?
4. Have you ever replied to a 'Lonely Hearts' ad? What happened?
5. Do you know anyone who has ever placed a 'Lonely Hearts' ad or replied to one? What happened? Was it a successful experience?

Reading

Read the passage and answer these questions:

1. What has the writer done?
2. Why has she done this?

NOT ONLY THE LONELY

Writer, 25, dark hair, brown eyes, GSOH, seeks reliable, intelligent, 30-something man for long walks, long conversations and long-term relationship. No time wasters.

OK. So I did it! But then everybody's doing it. There are over two million people registered with dating agencies – and that's the expensive way to do it. So there must be at least twice as many using 'Lonely Hearts' ads. The thing is, the men and women who place these ads aren't necessarily lonely. Take me, I'm not. I've got a wide circle of friends. And an active social life. It's just that my circle of friends does not include many single men. So, if I want to meet any single males I need to take positive action. My ad joined those of other professional women who do not have the time to follow the more usual methods of finding a partner and those of some of the 1.5 million single mothers who have obvious difficulties in getting out.

And was it a successful ad? Well, I think 75 replies speaks for itself! Some of the replies were touching; some were surprising, some appealing and some appalling. A few people clearly did not have sufficient self-knowledge to realise they were nerds. Others were, for a variety of reasons, clearly unsuitable. In the end I met 12. Of these, 7 were liars, usually much older, fatter or uglier than their photos suggested; two were nerds, missed at the initial examination. One was far too enthusiastic about putting his hand on my knee; one lived in Edinburgh, a beautiful city (and he was a nice man) but I wanted a long-term friend – not a long-distance one.

The last one I met was Gavin. 36, intelligent, good-looking, kind, definitely GSOH, and sitting across the table from me as I write this. Oh yes – and tomorrow he moves into my flat. I did it. And it works!

True or false?

Mark the following sentences T (true) or F (false):

1. The writer thinks that over four million people use 'Lonely Hearts' ads.
2. Most people who use 'Lonely Hearts' ads don't have many friends.
3. Professional women use the ads because they don't have much time for socialising.
4. Some people lied when they replied to the writer's ad.
5. She met her current partner through her ad.

Discussion

Discuss these questions in pairs or small groups:

1. What does the writer mean when she says 'I did it'?
2. Do you think the writer really does have a 'wide circle of friends'?
3. Are 'Lonely Hearts' ads popular in your country as a way of meeting new people?
4. How do you feel about people who place 'Lonely Hearts' ads? Do you think they are sad and lonely? Or are they just normal people who are too busy to meet the sort of people they would like to?
5. If you ever placed an ad or replied to one, would you lie about any of the following?
   a) your age   b) your appearance   c) your job   d) your income   e) your past

Language

Work in pairs. Put the sentences below in the correct order to make a story:

1.	Mark fancied Lucy.
☐	They got engaged.
☐	They got on very well.
☐	She had twin girls, Emma and Katie.
☐	Mark proposed to Lucy.
☐	They got married.
☐	Lucy got custody of the children.
☐	Lucy became pregnant.
☐	He asked her out on a date.
☐	Mark and Lucy started to have rows.
☐	They started going out together.
☐	They split up.
☐	They fell in love with each other.
☐	Lucy asked for a divorce.
☐	Mark had an affair.
☐	They went on their honeymoon.

Now use some of these expressions to tell a story which is true for you.

Discussion

1. Write a description of yourself in 25 words for a 'Lonely Hearts' ad. Put together the descriptions from everyone in the class and mix them up. Ask the teacher to read them out one at a time. Can you recognise the writers? Has anybody lied? Here are some typical expressions from these ads:

solvent lady	professional male	looking for fun	sincere and caring
own house	down to earth	intelligent guy	likes dancing
with own teeth	easy-going	strong body	biker
romantic	blue eyes	enjoys cinema	athletic

2. Discuss these questions in pairs or small groups:

a. In your country where do most people meet their partners?

in school/at work	in bars and nightclubs
at parties	through their family
through 'Lonely Hearts' ads	some other way

b. What do you think are the advantages and disadvantages of trying to make friends through a 'Lonely Hearts' ad?

c. Are there any dangers involved in meeting people through a 'Lonely Hearts' ad? What advice would you give a friend who told you (s)he was going out tonight on a lonely hearts date?

Newspapers

Discussion

Discuss these questions with your partner. Give further details where possible.

1. Have you ever …

   had your name mentioned in a newspaper?

   had your photo in a newspaper?

   written an article for a newspaper?

   had a photo you took published in a newspaper?

   had a letter published in a newspaper?

2. Which newspapers do you read? Do you read a paper every day?

3. Why do you read thatpaper / those particular papers?

Reading

Read these two articles, which report the same incident, and answer these questions:

1. What happened to Cara Phillips?
2. Who saved her?

MIRACLE ESCAPE

Cara Phillips, 11, daughter of top model Selina Phillips, had a miraculous escape yesterday whilst out on a school trip. Cara was swept away during a river activity in the rain-swollen River Wharfe in North Yorkshire.

Luckily her cries were heard by teacher Denise Carter, who pluckily plunged into the raging torrent. Grabbing young Cara, Ms Carter, 36, managed to avert an almost certain tragedy by dragging the terrified girl to the river bank. 'I am so grateful to Denise Carter,' said Cara's supermodel mum, Selina. 'Her quick-thinking and her courage saved my daughter's life. She's a wonderful woman.'

SCHOOL TRIP DISASTER AVOIDED

A school trip to the River Wharfe in North Yorkshire would have ended in disaster yesterday but for the courage of teacher Denise Carter.

The River Wharfe, running faster and deeper than usual after the recent heavy rains, swept away one of her pupils, Cara Phillips, aged 11. Ms Carter, hearing the girl's cries, bravely jumped into the water and pulled the girl to safety.

North Yorkshire police will today be questioning staff and pupils about the incident. They will be trying to decide whether the school had properly followed the guidelines for school trips, recently laid down by the government.

Language 1

Look again at the articles. Match the words and expressions on the left with the words and expressions on the right which convey a similar meaning. Note that the matches may not be exactly the same grammatically.

1. rain-swollen	a. bravely
2. pluckily	b. jumped
3. an almost certain tragedy	c. pulling the girl
4. plunged	d. a disaster
5. dragging the terrified girl	e. running faster than usual after recent heavy rain

Discussion

Read the articles again. Discuss these questions in pairs or small groups:

1. Which article uses the more colourful and emotive language?
2. Which article mentions Cara's mother? Why?
3. Which article has a quote from Cara's mother?
4. Which article is the more factual?
5. Which article looks at the wider picture and the consequences of what happened?
6. Which article is more concerned with news and which with 'human interest'?
7. Which is probably from a tabloid (or popular) newspaper and which from a 'quality' paper?
8. Which do you prefer?

Language 2

Complete these sentences with appropriate forms of the following words and phrases:

editor	TV guide
obituary	horoscope
crossword	proprietor
sports	headline
article	reviews

1. Have a look at my . . . . and tell me what it says for today, will you? I'm a Scorpio.
2. Did you know Jason Matthews had died? I saw his . . . . in the paper this morning.
3. I'm never able to do the . . . . in *The Independent*. It's just so difficult.
4. He's Canadian and I believe he was the first foreign . . . . of a British newspaper.
5. I'm staying in tonight. Throw me the . . . . I want to see if there's anything worth watching.
6. If you're keen on football and cricket, you ought to buy *The Daily Telegraph*. It has by far the best . . . . news.
7. When I saw the . . . . , I thought there'd been another plane crash, but then I read the . . . . and realised it had just been delayed for 24 hours!
8. I don't think I'll bother seeing the new Fred Durkin movie. The . . . . were terrible.
9. I was so angry about the government's plans to raise taxes that I wrote to the . . . . of *The Times*. My letter was published yesterday morning. Did you see it?

Discussion

1. Write down the names of 6 or 7 daily newspapers in your country. Work in pairs. Explain to your partner the following:

1. Which have the biggest circulation?
2. Which are local, regional, or national?
3. Which are tabloid (popular and sensational)?
4. Which are considered to be 'quality' papers?
5. Which contain the best news reporting?
6. Which contain the most gossip?
7. Which contain the best sports reporting?
8. Which do you read regularly?

2. Work in groups of four. Choose one of the headlines below. Divide into two pairs. One pair writes a short article from a tabloid newspaper about the headline; the other pair writes a short article from a quality newspaper about the headline. Compare your articles.

> **PRINCESS HITS PHOTOGRAPHER**

> **MP'S PAST COMES TO LIGHT**

> **QUEEN'S PRIVATE LETTERS SHOCK**

> **TEACHER TO MARRY STUDENT**

To tip or not to tip?

Discussion

Discuss these questions with a partner:

1. Is it normal to tip in your country?
2. When? How much should you give?
3. Do you always tip when you should?
4. How much do you give?
5. Have you had any good or bad experiences when tipping?

Did you know?

In the 18th century, coffee houses in Britain had a box on each table. A notice on each box read: *To Insure Promptness.* Customers were encouraged to put money in the box for better service. Soon the money became known by its initials: TIP.

Reading

Read the statements below. Decide if you agree or disagree with each one. Then compare what you think with your partner.

I never tip. Employers should pay their staff a decent wage. If they don't, the staff should leave.

I only tip if I know I'm going back somewhere. Otherwise, there's no point.

I never know what to do. If my taxi fare comes to £10, I just give the driver £10. But if it comes to £6 or £7, I tell them to keep the change. They must think I'm mad!

I hate it when porters carry my bags to my room in hotels – and then they hang around waiting for a tip.

I eat out a lot on business. I've had excellent service and truly awful service. I don't want trouble. I leave a 10% tip, no matter what the service has been like. Just to be on the safe side.

Where I come from, everyone thinks we're tight with money. That's nonsense! I tip everyone everywhere – just to try and break down people's prejudices about us.

I only tip taxi drivers and hairdressers if they chat to me. I reckon it's part of their job. No talk, no tip!

If I've just had a very expensive meal, I never leave a tip. I don't see why I should pay through the nose twice!

Language

Complete the following expressions from the quotes:

1. We wouldn't need to tip if employers paid a . . . . wage.
2. I don't like to offend so I always tip – just to be on the . . . . side!
3. Some people have the reputation of being . . . . with their money.
4. I hate it when I hear people saying, "Just keep the . . . .". It's so patronising.
5. There's no . . . . in tipping people you're never going to see again in your life!
6. I never tip – no . . . . what the service has been like. I just don't do it on principle.
7. I don't think one person can . . . . down prejudices which are hundreds of years old.
8. In expensive restaurants you're paying through the . . . . anyway!

Go back and underline the complete expressions in the examples above.

Discussion

Who would you tip? Tick the appropriate boxes:

	Yes	No	Maybe
1. a waiter in a coffee shop	☐	☐	☐
2. a waiter in an expensive restaurant	☐	☐	☐
3. a hairdresser	☐	☐	☐
4. a taxi driver	☐	☐	☐
5. your dentist	☐	☐	☐
6. an assistant in a high street burger bar	☐	☐	☐
7. a steward on an aeroplane	☐	☐	☐
8. a hotel porter	☐	☐	☐
9. the person who conducts your wedding ceremony	☐	☐	☐
10. your doctor	☐	☐	☐
11. a tour guide	☐	☐	☐
12. a hotel chambermaid	☐	☐	☐

Work in pairs and compare your answers.

Now discuss these questions with your partner:

a. Should tipping be made illegal – after all, it's just an excuse for employers to pay less?
b. Should tips in a restaurant be pooled and shared between all the waiters? Or should each waiter keep his or her own tips?
c. In Britain a recent court ruling says that tips added to a bill and paid for by credit card belong to the employer – not the waiter. Do you think this is fair?
d. In Britain tips are taxed. Do you think this is fair?

What do you say?

What do you think British people say when they tip? Tick the expressions you think are possible:

☐ "Thanks for everything."
☐ "Here's something. Buy yourself a drink."
☐ "Keep the change."
☐ "Here's your ten per cent."
☐ "Here you are and thank you very much."
☐ Nothing.

Royalty

Discussion

Discuss these questions in pairs or small groups:

1. Does your country have a monarch or a president?
2. Who is the head of state at the moment?
3. What real power does the head of state have in your country?
4. Do you think they are doing a good job or not? Why?
5. Have you ever met the head of state of your country? When? In what circumstances?

*"It's a **really** nice area."*

Reading

Read the article below and answer these questions:

1. Which piece of information do you find most surprising? Why?
2. Did any of the items make you laugh? Which? Why?
3. Compare your answers in pairs or small groups.

TEN THINGS YOU DIDN'T KNOW ABOUT THE QUEEN

• As reigning monarch, she has the right of ownership of all the mute swans on the River Thames. This right has been handed down from medieval times. She is also the only person in Britain allowed by law to eat swan.

• When she gives people presents of photographs of herself and her husband, the frame is an indication of the status of the recipient. Silver frames are for Presidents; blue leather frames are the next best; then brown. Domestic staff receive unframed photos.

• A recent opinion poll on the popularity of the royal family, compiled at the Queen's own request, discovered that 'fewer than 1 in 4 people thinks they are hard-working and only 1 in 10 thinks they are good value for money.'

• In the year 2000 she stayed in a three-bedroom suite in the Principe di Savoia hotel in Milan. It cost £4,300 a night. She hired an extra room just for her shoes.

• She has a plastic duck and a small crown in her bath.

• Her personal wealth was recently estimated at £300 million. She and her husband are now the only members of the royal family who receive money from the state.

• She uses special black blotting paper so that no state or personal secrets are revealed.

• She enjoys doing jigsaws and rents them from a jigsaw club.

• She also enjoys Scrabble and surfing the internet. Apparently, she never reads books unless they are about horses.

• It is said that she strangles pheasants while shooting in Scotland.

True or false?

Mark the following sentences T (true) or F (false):

1. No one except the Queen is allowed to eat swan.
2. The Queen has a large number of shoes.
3. The Queen no longer receives money from the state.
4. The Queen uses a fountain pen.
5. The Queen enjoys reading.

Discussion

Discuss these questions in pairs or small groups:

1. Which of the following opinions best sums up your country's view of the British royals?
   They're really interesting.   *The Queen's great, but we're not interested in her family.*
   They're all so boring.   *Come on, it's the 21st century we're living in – not the 18th!*
2. Can you read about them regularly in newspapers and magazines?
3. What sort of articles are written about them?
4. How do they compare with other royal families? For example, the Dutch, Spanish, or Swedish?
5. Do you feel the British royal family is a worthwhile institution or a waste of money?
6. If members of a royal family were visiting a town in your country near where you live, would you go to see them? Why/Why not?

Language

Make more expressions from the boxes.

abolish	a republic
appoint	a government
elect	a prime minister
found	the monarchy

opinion	wealth
election	family
royal	campaign
personal	poll

Complete this text using the correct form of complete expressions from the boxes above:

A recent . . . . (1) showed that the . . . . (2) in Erefaria was not at all popular on account of their enormous . . . . (3). A national movement soon rose up demanding to . . . . (4) . Fearing for their lives, the king and his immediate family fled the country. The army briefly took control, but the leading generals decided the best way forward for the country as a whole was to . . . . (5). The first . . . . (6) went smoothly and less than a year after the departure of the king, the people . . . . (7) for the first time.

Discussion

Mark these opinions – agree / disagree / don't have an opinion. Then compare your responses in pairs or in small groups.

	agree	disagree	no opinion
• I'd rather have a president than a monarch. At least you can get rid of a president if you don't like them.	☐	☐	☐
• The problem with having a president is that it's a political office. If you have a monarch they are above politics.	☐	☐	☐
• If Britain got rid of its monarchy, tabloid journalists would have nothing to write about.	☐	☐	☐
• Having a monarchy is very old fashioned. We're living in the 21st century now – we ought to get rid of these ancient institutions.	☐	☐	☐
• I think it's terrible that someone should become a king or a queen just because of an accident of birth.	☐	☐	☐
• Just think of the amount of money spent on a presidential election campaign. What a waste!	☐	☐	☐
• Monarchy equals continuity – that's a major advantage, to my mind.	☐	☐	☐

Fashion

Discussion

Work in pairs or small groups. Discuss these questions:

1. What sort of clothes do you wear most of the time?
2. Do you wear different clothes for work/study? In what way are they different?
3. What do you wear for more formal occasions and for parties?
4. Where do you buy most of your clothes?
5. Do you buy designer label clothes? Which designers?
6. Do you read any fashion magazines? Which?

Reading

Read the article. Match each of the summaries below to one of the paragraphs in the article:

Summary	Paragraph number
What people wear and don't wear today	___
What fashion designers do	___
A very special dress	___

FASHION! – WHAT'S THE POINT?

1. Björk is on the catwalk. Her skirt is made of bright red ostrich feathers. The 2,000 shiny red glass beads attached to her top ring like little bells. She sounds like a one-person bell orchestra. And the beads are not just ordinary beads. They are specially-ordered microscope slides, each individually hand-drilled and individually painted red. Extraordinary? Yes. Radical? Yes. But what's the point?

2. This is the 21st century after all. Most people are happy with a T-shirt and jeans, a shirt and a pair of chinos. Even business executives dress down these days. Clothes are casual: easy to wear, easy to care for. Whereas the dress that Björk wore, designed by Alexander McQueen, took over a month to make and is one of only two in existence. The other is in an exhibition in a museum in London. Though, frankly, who else would want one?

3. For many people extreme fashion is just self-indulgence on the part of the designers. They are attention seekers, they make headlines, but they don't sell clothes. But for the designers themselves, fashion is a way of airing ideas, of making a statement. The clothes they design are intended to provoke and challenge the way we live, think and are. Closer to conceptual art and less to do with the clothes industry, perhaps.

Questions in pairs

Work in pairs. Read the article again. Then take turns asking each other the following questions:

1. What is Björk's skirt made of?
2. What is Björk's top made of?
3. What do most people like to wear these days?
4. How do many business executives dress these days?
5. How many dresses have been made like the one Björk is wearing?
6. How many people does the writer think would like a dress like Björk's?
7. How do many people feel about fashion designers?
8. How do fashion designers see their work?

Discussion

Discuss your reactions to these questions with a partner:

1. How do you think Björk's outfit sounds?
   brilliant   *outrageous*   *decadent*

2. If you arrived at a party and someone was wearing a dress like that, what would you think?
   How embarrassing!   *Where can I get one?*   *What a waste of money!*

3. What would you say if you were introduced to them?
   I just love your frock.   *What ARE you wearing?*   *Who's your designer?*

Do you think extraordinary clothes really do challenge the way we live? Why? Why not?

Are fashion designers attention seekers or artists?

Language

Cross out the word in each of the boxes which is not a natural collocation:

street current passing factory high	fashion

be in come back into leave go out of follow	fashion

Complete the sentences below with the correct form of a word or expression from the boxes:

1. You must get some new sunglasses. Those ones . . . . fashion about five years ago.
2. The clothing industry has gone crazy this year. Everything from sports clothes to . . . . . . fashion.
3. Alan must spend a fortune on clothes. Whatever he wears . . . . always . . . . fashion.
4. You don't see supermodels with rings in their nose or their eyebrow. It's very much . . . . . fashion.
5. I reckon I could wear my 60s tie-dyed T-shirts again now. They seem to have . . . . fashion.
6. Everyone's wearing orange this summer. I'm sure it's just a . . . . fashion.

Discussion

Complete this questionnaire on your own first:

How fashion conscious are you?
Fill in the table below with appropriate brand/designer names.

	brands you own	you would like to own	you would never wear
jeans	. . . .	. . . .	. . . .
T-shirts	. . . .	. . . .	. . . .
jeans	. . . .	. . . .	. . . .
trainers	. . . .	. . . .	. . . .
dress / suit	. . . .	. . . .	. . . .

And fashion isn't just about clothes! It's about other lifestyle things.

	brands you own	brands you would like to own	brands you would never buy
watch	. . . .	. . . .	. . . .
mobile	. . . .	. . . .	. . . .
CD player	. . . .	. . . .	. . . .
car	. . . .	. . . .	. . . .
computer	. . . .	. . . .	. . . .

Compare your answers in groups. Then vote for the person in your class who is the most / least fashion conscious.

Is it right to eat meat?

Discussion

First answer these questions on your own:

1. Are you vegetarian?
2. Do you eat meat? How often?
3. Do you eat fish? How often?
4. Do you know any vegetarians?
5. Do you know why they are vegetarian?
6. Are there many vegetarian restaurants where you live?

Compare your answers in pairs or small groups.

Reading

Read the texts below and answer these questions.
According to the texts which person:

   a. enjoys eating meat?
   b. has been a vegetarian for a long time?
   c. enjoys watching animals?
   d. thinks the other is a hypocrite?

"Their protective colouring sometimes makes them very difficult to hit."

IS IT RIGHT TO EAT MEAT?

YES

Some people think that in an ideal world we would all be vegetarians. A lot of poor unfortunate animals would therefore be able to enjoy their lives without the prospect of needless suffering and a premature death. But the way I look at it is this. If we didn't eat meat, no one would keep sheep, cows or any other animals that provide food. We would never be able to enjoy watching young lambs and calves playing in the fields. Instead of trying to encourage people to do something which seems rather unnatural, why don't we try and make sure that food animals are treated well? Being vegetarian really isn't necessary. Let's just treat our animals with a bit of kindness and respect.

NO

It seems a bit hypocritical to preach for the better treatment of animals – only to kill them and eat them! Of course we don't need to eat meat. I'm 82 years old and I've been a vegetarian since I was 25. What's more, I'm extremely fit and active. In fact, I ran the London Marathon last year. Some people seem to think it's natural to eat meat – but that's not so. Sure, we used to eat meat in the past, but that was before we knew how to grow enough fruit and vegetables. Anyway, not even all animals are vegetarian. Look at elephants, for example, they live on grass and hay; they are enormously strong; and they live to a great age.

Discussion

Discuss these questions in pairs or small groups:

1. Do animals really 'face the prospect' of a premature death?
2. Are they ever aware that they are destined to be eaten?
3. What do you think would happen to sheep, cows etc. if:
   a. the number of vegetarians increased dramatically?
   b. everyone was vegetarian?
4. How well are food animals treated in your country?
5. Are you happy with the way they are treated?
6. Do you think it is hypocritical to treat animals well and then kill them and eat them?
7. Do you think it is really 'necessary' or 'natural' to eat meat?

Language

Underline the following words and phrases in the text and notice how they are used:

the way I look at it is this   *of course*   *what's more*
sure, ... but ...   *anyway*   *for example*

Now use these expressions to complete the following situations:

1. I've got a few friends who are vegetarians and they drive me mad sometimes. . . . . ,
   when I invite them round for a meal, I always make something which is vegetarian, but when they
   invite me back, they never cook meat for me!

2. I know all the arguments, but . . . . – it's a symptom of the
   growing affluence of society. Ask someone who is starving in Africa which they would rather
   do – die or eat an animal. I know what their answer would be!
   > . . . . . . that's understandable, ... we're not in their situation and we have a choice.

3. . . . . we need a balanced diet! It's perfectly possible to be a vegetarian and
   eat healthily. I'm not so sure about a vegan diet, however. Vegans always seem to look pale
   and in need of a good steak!

4. I haven't eaten meat for almost 40 years and . . . . I don't intend changing my
   fundamental belief that it is cruel to eat another creature.

5. I always buy organic food. I just can't bear the thought of eating all the pesticides they spray
   on fruit and vegetables.
   > I agree with you. I hate the thought of what they do to our food. You're absolutely right.
   . . . . , there's not much I can do. I can't actually afford to buy organic stuff, so in
   the end I don't really have a choice.

Discussion

Complete the questionnaire below, then compare your answers in pairs or small groups.

HOW CONCERNED ARE YOU?

Answer the following questions. Then add up your score at the end.

1. **Do you buy genetically modified foods?**
   a. Never.
   b. Only if there is no alternative.
   c. It doesn't make any difference to me if they
      are GM or not.

2. **Given the choice between organic and non-organic foods, what do you do?**
   a. I always buy the organic option.
   b. I sometimes buy the organic option – unless
      it is much more expensive.
   c. I always buy the non-organic option – it's
      usually cheaper.

3. **When you buy eggs, how often do you get free range eggs?**
   a. Always.
   b. Sometimes.
   c. Never.

4. **What sort of fish do you buy?**
   a. I never eat fish.
   b. I usually buy wild fish.
   c. I usually buy farmed fish.

5. **Do you grow your own vegetables?**
   a. Yes.
   b. No, but a friend does and he gives me some.
   c. No.

6. **Where do you buy most of your food?**
   a. from local farmers.
   b. from local markets.
   c. from supermarkets.

7. **What sort of produce do you generally buy?**
   a. Mostly fresh.
   b. About half fresh, half tinned or frozen.
   c. Mostly tinned or frozen or ready to cook.

Less than 11: Do you care at all about what you eat? You really must start giving it some thought.

11 – 13: You could do much better but at least you have some good habits. You really must try and improve.

14–18: Not too bad but you could do better. Think about ways to improve what you eat.

19 or more: Well done! You are very concerned about the quality of what you eat. Try to persuade others to be like you.

Score 3 for each a; 2 for each b; and 1 for each c.

How did you score?

The exploitation of animals

Discussion

Tick the items in the list below that you have seen:

1. horse-racing ❐
2. dog-racing ❐
3. performing animals in a circus ❐
4. a bullfight ❐
5. animals in a zoo ❐
6. a dog fight ❐

7. show jumping ❐
8. a dog show ❐
9. a fox hunt ❐
10. a cock fight ❐
11. a performing bear or monkey ❐
12. a pheasant shoot ❐

Compare your answers in pairs or small groups.

Reading

Read the two texts below. Which is pro bullfighting? Which is against it?

Text 1

Bullfighting is not just a sport; it is much more than that. For many Spaniards the bullfight is a proud part of their heritage. It is an art form which reflects the most basic issue to face man – namely, survival and domination of the wild. It is a ceremony which stirs up a variety of rich emotions: joy, danger, and glory. As a result, bullfighters are celebrated as national heroes participating in a dangerous ritual which at any moment may cut short their fame or even their life. Far from losing popularity, more and more people flock to bullfights in celebration of a uniquely national tradition.

Text 2

A bullfight may be a fight, but it's not a fair fight. The bull has little chance of defending itself, even less to survive. Do you know what happens before a fight? No? Read on.

• There are reports that many bulls are beaten and have heavy weights hung round their necks for weeks before a fight. They are already tired when they enter the arena.

• Bulls are kept in darkness for 48 hours before a fight. When they go out into the arena they are therefore blinded by the sunlight.

• Many bulls' horns have a few centimetres illegally cut off. This impairs their co-ordination and prevents them from navigating properly.

• Rather than being a clean kill, the bull is tormented and tired out before the matador finally attempts to kill it.

• Often the result of a bullfight is not immediate death, but just excessive mutilation. The final death blow, which is supposed to sever the spinal column, frequently fails and a fully conscious but paralysed beast is dragged from the arena.

• Bulls are not the only victims. Horses are often drugged and blindfolded before being taken into the arena. Their vocal cords are sometimes cut so that their cries cannot be heard by the crowd.

Questions in pairs

With a partner, take turns to ask and answer the following questions about the texts:

1. What do Spaniards feel that bullfighting symbolises?
2. How are bullfighters treated in Spain?
3. How popular is bullfighting in Spain nowadays? Why is this so?
4. What happens to bulls in the 48 hours before a fight? Why?
5. How do bulls 'navigate'?
6. Are bulls always killed cleanly in a bullfight? Why not?
7. Do other animals suffer in bullfights?
8. What animals suffer and how?

Discussion

Discuss these questions in pairs or small groups:

1. How far do you sympathise with the Spanish view of bullfighting?
2. Do you think bullfighting is an acceptable 'sport' or should it be banned?
3. Should the EU be allowed to make bullfighting illegal in Spain, or not?

Language

Here are 10 expressions to use during a discussion. Complete the sentences using these words:

minute	*stick*	*take*	*interrupt*	*listen*
clearly	*another*	*something*	*misunderstood*	*point*

1. I think you've got the wrong end of the . . . . . . here actually.
2. Why don't you shut up and . . . . . . for a minute?
3. I think you've . . . . . . what I was trying to say.
4. If I could just say . . . . . . at this point ...
5. Just a . . . . I'd like to come in here if I may.
6. No, that's not my . . . . . . at all. What I'm trying to say is ...
7. Sorry, but I must . . . . . . you there.
8. Perhaps I haven't put this very . . . . What I mean is ...
9. That's not the point at all. Look. Let me put it . . . . . . way.
10. I'm afraid I have to . . . . . . you up on that point.

Which ones would you use to correct someone?
Which ones would you use to make a positive contribution to a discussion?
Which of the expressions are rude?

Discussion

Where do you draw the line? Do you agree or disagree with these statements? Discuss them in pairs or small groups. Try to use the expressions from the Language activity above.

> Horse-racing and dog-racing should be banned. They are not useful activities, they are just two different ways of getting gamblers to spend money.

> It seems odd that 'sports' in which one animal fights another (like cock fighting or dog fighting) are illegal in most countries. After all, these animals fight each other in the wild. The sports should all be made legal.

> Fox hunting is just another form of pest control. Nobody worries about killing rats. There are too many foxes and they need to be killed. Fox hunting is as good a way as any to do it. If people want to dress up in red jackets and have a party at the same time, that's their business.

> 36 million pheasants were bred in Britain last year just for the start of the pheasant shooting season. Most hunters do not eat the birds they kill so the majority of the dead birds are buried in specially dug holes. This is a disgrace and should be stopped immediately.

> Performing animals in circuses are unacceptable these days and yet people seem quite happy about show jumping. Show jumping horses are nothing more than performing animals. The sport should be banned.

> Dog shows should be banned. They humiliate dogs. There is nothing more offensive than seeing some of these dogs being shampooed and treated as if they were children.

Why get married?

Discussion

Discuss these questions with a partner:

1. In your opinion, what are the three commonest reasons people decide to get married?
2. Do you think marriage is 'a thing of the past'?
3. Do you know someone who has had a long and happy marriage? Why has it lasted?
4. Why do you think there is such a high divorce rate in many developed countries?
5. Are married people treated differently from single people in your experience? In what ways?

Share your opinions with the rest of the class.

Reading

Read this newspaper article and answer the questions below in pairs or small groups:

LAST TO MARRY WINS!

A group of unmarried male friends in New Jersey made a strange bet 20 years ago when they were all still at high school. They drew up a contract and set up a special bank account to hold the money they had each bet.

The pot of money grew until it was several thousand dollars and John Cheney was the lucky winner – because he is now the group's last remaining bachelor. He collected his winnings from his friends at a pub last Saturday. "I guess I just haven't found the right person," said Cheney, now 38 years old.

The whole story started when two of the group bet a six-pack of beer over which one would be the last to get married. The group eventually grew to nine men, all 1981 graduates of Haddonfield Memorial High School.

"We all thought we'd be bachelors for a long time," said Mike Koontz, also 38. He was the first member of the group to get married, walking down the aisle in 1987. He always thought John would win the money. "He's a real confirmed bachelor," said Mike.

1. What was the prize?
2. Why hasn't Cheney got married?
3. Why did they make the bet?

Do you think a group of young women would have made the same bet?
Was John Cheney's wait worth it?
What is a 'confirmed bachelor'?

"Belinda, will you make me the happiest man in the world and divorce me?"

Language

Divide the following expressions into two groups:

      B = before marriage   A = after marriage

1. go on honeymoon	12. propose to them
2. meet someone you like	13. have an affair with someone
3. talk about marriage	14. walk down the aisle
4. become friends	15. get engaged
5. get pregnant	16. start going out with them
6. meet their family	17. see a marriage counsellor
7. plan the wedding	18. get separated
8. have a stag / hen night	19. get divorced
9. have kids	20. find someone attractive
10. bring up children	21. start to get close
11. start having marriage problems	22. get back together again

With a partner, choose 10 of the expressions in the box and put them in the ideal order for you.

Discussion

1. In 2002, Rutgers University in the US released the results of a study which lists the top 10 reasons men are waiting longer these days to get married. In pairs or groups, discuss if you think each is a valid argument.

TOP 10 REASONS WHY MEN ARE RELUCTANT TO COMMIT TO MARRIAGE

1. They can have sex outside marriage more easily than in the past.
2. They can enjoy the benefits of having a wife by cohabiting rather than marrying.
3. They want to avoid divorce and its financial risks.
4. They want to wait until they are older to have children.
5. They are afraid that marriage will require too many changes and compromises.
6. They are waiting for the perfect soulmate, and she hasn't yet appeared.
7. In the US there are few social pressures to marry.
8. They are reluctant to marry a woman who already has children.
9. They want to own a house before they get a wife.
10. They want to enjoy life as a single man as long as they can.

2. With a partner, choose one of the following situations. Prepare your part in the conversation for 2 minutes, then have the conversation.

a. Your son/daughter is now 30 and you want them to settle down. Try to talk them into it.

b. You have been going out with your partner for 3 years and are looking for a bigger commitment. Try to persuade them to think about getting married.

c. Your best friend is deciding whether or not to get married. Try to talk them into it.

d. Your best friend is deciding whether or not to get married. Try to talk them out of it.

Intercultural problems

With a partner, discuss the following:

1. Would you consider marrying (or are you already married to) someone from another country or culture?
2. What special problems do you think arise from a marriage between people from different countries or cultures?
3. Make a list of the benefits and drawbacks of such marriages.

I hate my boss!

Discussion

In pairs or small groups, discuss the following questions:

1. Have you ever had a boss you didn't like? Why didn't you like him/her?
2. Do you think it is simply expected that people dislike their boss?
3. Which of the following would you do if you didn't like your boss:
   a. resign and find another job?
   b. discuss your problem with your boss?
   c. go to the personnel department and raise the matter with them?
   d. talk to your closest colleagues?
   e. ignore the problem and hope your boss will leave?
   f. something else?

Reading

Read the complaints below from a popular website. Decide which problem you most sympathise with. Have you or someone you know ever been in any of these situations?

1. MY BOSS IS A SLAVE DRIVER.
I work as a personal assistant and I have a boss who is in love with her job! Of course she is! She owns the place! The trouble is she expects us to love the job as much as she does! I'm sorry, if it's 6 o'clock, I'm going home! By then I've had enough!

2. WHY CAN'T I DO ANYTHING RIGHT?
I can't take it any more! My boss must have a list somewhere of everything I do wrong. He waits for the exact moment when I do something and then – out of nowhere there he is! He's always on my back about the same things. He never says anything nice or encouraging.

3. I SHOULD BE DOING HER JOB!
I don't know how much more of this I can stand. I can see the company I work for going downhill because my boss is so incompetent. I don't know how she got her job! She doesn't know what she's doing!

4. I DO ALL THE WORK AND HE GETS ALL THE CREDIT.
I can't believe my boss sometimes. I do all the work and he takes all the credit. He basically says 'do this' and 'do that'. Then, when the work gets noticed, he doesn't say it was me. He lets people assume that he did the work! I'm sick of this!

5. PLEASE DON'T BE MY FRIEND!
Oh, please. Give me a break! I am so tired of my boss pretending she's our friend. I mean, come on! She's our boss! She comes into the staffroom during our breaks trying to take part in our conversations and share in bits of gossip. I'm sorry, but somebody who is doing half the work I'm doing and getting twice the pay does not deserve equal status with me.

6. IF YOU DON'T TRUST ME, THEN DON'T HIRE ME!
I'm finished with my job. My boss doesn't trust me or anyone else at work. If he sees me on the phone, he tries to listen in to see if the call is work-related. He walks past people working at computer terminals to see if he can catch them playing games! Last week I even caught him checking people's desks for – goodness knows what! He's a creep!

Compare your answers and share your stories.

Discussion

Discuss these questions in pairs or small groups:

1. Which of the six situations did you think was the worst one?
2. Did any of them seem 'silly' to you? Which ones?
3. Which ones have very obvious solutions? What advice would you give?
4. Do you think all the people should just leave their jobs?
5. What would you do if you heard one of these complaints at work and realised it was referring to you?

Language

1. Each situation had an expression in it that means the person could take no more. Find the missing word to complete these sentences:

1. I'm . . . . . . of this.
2. I can't . . . . . . it any more.
3. Give me a . . . . . . !
4. I'm finished . . . . . . my job.
5. I've had . . . . . . !
6. I don't know how much more of this I can . . . .

2. Do you have equivalents for these expressions in your language? Work with a partner and translate them.

Discussion

So what makes a good boss and what makes a bad boss?

1. Work in two groups. One group should make a list of what makes a good boss, the other should list what makes a bad boss.

GOOD BOSSES	BAD BOSSES
1. A good boss is someone who	1. A bad boss is someone who . . . .
2. A good boss always	2. A bad boss always . . . .
3. A good boss never	3. A bad boss never . . . .
4. Some characteristics of a good boss:	4. Some characteristics of a bad boss:

2. When you finish, find a student who made the opposite list and compare. Do you agree?

Are good bosses like good teachers? Talk about the parallels and the differences.

Scams – how can people be so stupid?

Discussion

1. Look at this list of ways to spend your money. Tick the sensible ones:

- ☐ a college or university education
- ☐ a new car
- ☐ renting a flat
- ☐ yoga classes
- ☐ a big traditional wedding

- ☐ the lottery
- ☐ a new house
- ☐ getting your palm read
- ☐ psychic readings
- ☐ playing the stock market

2. Compare the items you ticked in pairs or small groups. Give some other good ways to spend money? And bad ones?

Reading

Read this quote and discuss the questions below in pairs:

> 'For years my wife and I saved our money. We didn't have any kids. We were going to spend the money enjoying our retirement. But then she died. I was devastated. Maybe that's why they found it so easy. It must have been like taking candy from a baby.'

1. How old do you think the person who said this is?
2. Who is the 'they' he refers to?
3. What do you think 'taking candy from a baby' means?

Now read this man's story and answer the questions below:

Had – Part 1

George Stockton, 72, of Wheeling, West Virginia, has become the latest victim in a rise in money-making scams aimed at the elderly. Stockton says a woman approached him with an offer to 'put him back in touch' with his deceased wife. "I do miss her so, so much. The psychic offered me a new chance," lamented Stockton, his eyes watering. "I guess I was taken in by that." The woman, who Stockton says he met at bingo, talked him into visiting her house where, for a fee of $50 initially, she would receive 'messages' from his departed wife, Linda. "She seemed to know so much about her. I thought it had to be real," George recalls. "She lured me in and I fell for it, hook, line and sinker." The initial $50 fee increased to $100. The psychic insisted that she needed to buy more special materials, and that each session took more work, requiring higher fees. She had already managed to con him out of over $7,000. At one point, George nearly gave up.

1. Is this kind of thing uncommon?
2. How did George Stockton know the woman?

Before continuing to read Part 2, discuss this question in pairs or small groups: What do you think happens next?

Had – Part 2

I said, "Enough. That's too expensive. I've paid too much money already!" That's when she offered to do an 'incarnation.' The 'incarnation' would allow Linda's spirit to enter her body. According to the psychic, this would allow him to speak directly to Linda, as if she was really there in the room with him. "This was an offer I could not refuse. I paid her the money." The 'money' George refers to was his life savings of $48,000. "It's all gone now. I have nowhere to go. I've been had!" Police are still searching for the scam artist.

3. Why did she suddenly offer an 'incarnation'?
4. How much money did she manage to get from George?
5. How much money does he have left?
6. Is what she did illegal? Does this happen in your country?

Discussion

Discuss these questions in pairs or small groups:

1. Do you think the psychic specifically chose George Stockton? Why?
2. What techniques did she use to make him give her money?
3. The psychic managed to take over $50,000 in the end from George, and now the police are after her. But what if she had stopped at just $500? Or $50? Should it be illegal?

Language

Go back to the article and underline expressions that mean 'to fool someone'. Compare with a partner. Then use the expressions you underlined to complete these dialogues:

Dialogue 1

A: Is that your new car?
B: Yes, that's right.
A: How much did you pay for it?
B: $15,000.
A: You've . . . . !

Dialogue 2

A: You're getting married, George?
B: I'm afraid so.
A: Well, how did that happen?
B: I don't know exactly. Somehow, she . . . . it.

Dialogue 3

A: So, are you coming fishing?
B: Yes. I called in sick. I told him I had an 'extremely contagious' virus.
A: Do you think he . . . . it?
B: I certainly hope so!

Dialogue 4

A: Have fun in Las Vegas. But be careful!
B: Why?
A: It's very easy to be . . . . all the noise and excitement and spend a fortune!

Discussion

1. George Stockton's sad case is perhaps an extreme one. Have you ever felt you've been 'had'? What happened?

2. Look at these situations. Do you consider them scams?

cigarette advertising
home contents insurance
beauty products
sales in shops
double-glazing offers
revolutionary diets
spending on defence
psychotherapy
alternative medicine
self-help books
anti-ageing creams
cosmetic surgery
pet funerals
cures for baldness

3. Can you think of any others? Discuss in pairs, then as a class.

"It worked! We've sent each one home with a gerbil."

Bad habits

Discussion

Discuss these questions with a partner:

1. Do you have any habits which you consider bad habits?
2. Do you have any old habits that you can't give up?
3. Did you use to have a bad habit that you've given up? How did you do it?
4. Are there any bad habits in other people that really annoy you?

Share your ideas with the rest of the class.

Reading

Read about these people with unusually anti-social habits and answer the questions below. Which one is the strangest? What do they all have in common?

154 TONS OF RUBBISH FOUND IN SPANIARD'S HOME

SAN SEBASTIAN DE LOS REYES, Spain (AP) – Workers with heavy equipment have removed 154 tons of rubbish from a man's home outside Madrid. The job took two weeks to complete. 58-year-old Antonio Villalba refused repeated requests from neighbours and city officials to clean up his yard and house. It stank and there were rats in and around the house, the newspaper *El País* said. The house was so packed with everything from tin cans to car parts that Villalba was forced to live in a tiny compartment in the back and reached it through a tunnel he made in the rubbish. Villalba, a widower who lived alone, was taken to a nursing home until the job was completed.

DOZENS OF DEAD CATS DISCOVERED IN HOME OF EX-COP

COOPER CITY, Fla. (AP) – A former police officer was arrested after authorities found 67 dead cats and dozens of other neglected felines at a house authorities said was used as an 'animal retreat'. Police said the dead cats were in the woman's refrigerator and freezer, some in plastic bags. Another 24 cats, many of them underfed, were also found. "It was foul, believe me," said police Capt. Marvin E. Stoner Jr. Audrey Weed, 50, was charged with animal abandonment and was awaiting trial. Neighbours said Weed had a soft spot for abandoned animals and habitually brought them home, but became overwhelmed.

MAN FOUND DEAD AT HOME – LIZARDS EATING HIS BODY

DOVER, Del (AP) – Several pet lizards were found eating the corpse of their owner in his apartment, police said. Police were called to Ronald Huff's apartment in Newark, Del. on Wednesday after he failed to show up for work, investigators said. Huff, 42, lived alone and had last been seen on Sunday. Seven Nile monitor lizards, the largest measuring 6 feet long, were recovered and brought to the SPCA. Director John Caldwell said that the lizards are "alive and well". He added that one of the reptiles recovered was acting aggressively, "actually going towards you – mouth open."

Discussion

Discuss these questions in pairs or small groups:

1. Why did the authorities go to Antonio Villalba's house?
2. How do you know it was a big job?
3. Were all the cats in Audrey Weed's apartment found dead?
4. Why do you think someone would keep all those cats?
5. Do you think Ronald Huff was killed by his lizards?
6. What size were the lizards?

Language

1. The following expressions are common ways to talk about habits. Underline the verbs.

a. It's a hard habit to break.
b. I'm trying to cut down.
c. I've been meaning to give up.
d. Once you start, you can't stop.

Do you have equivalents in your language?

2. Match the following to complete the bad habits:

1. bite your   a. fingers
2. crack your   b. knuckles
3. grind your   c. nose
4. pick your   d. teeth
5. snap your   e. hair
6. play with your   f. nails

Discussion

Work in pairs or small groups. What habits do the following refer to?

1. I'm down to two packs a day now.
2. OK, just a drop.
3. My nails never grow.
4. Get your finger out of there!
5. He stays up all night watching.
6. I get on and I can't get off – I just surf all day long.
7. I just can't throw things out.
8. I can't resist a bargain.
9. I have a terrible sweet tooth.

"Hoarder!"

Questionnaire – are you a hoarder?

Are you a hoarder? Do you find it impossible to throw things out? For some people, such as Antonio Villalba in the article, this is a real problem – now officially recognised by doctors as an obsessive-compulsive disorder. Some people find it impossible to throw anything away – even hoarding used bottles, empty cereal packets, etc. But aren't we all in some small way secret hoarders? Tick which of the following things you secretly hoard:

☐ ordinary plastic carrier bags

☐ carrier bags from famous shops

☐ empty wine bottles

☐ empty jam jars

☐ old newspapers

☐ old magazines

☐ favourite old clothes

☐ programmes from concerts or plays

☐ pens

☐ old cosmetics

Find other people in the class who share your weakness. Are there other things which you are willing to admit to hoarding?

Killed by a flying duck!

Discussion

Work in pairs. Rate the following everyday activities on a health-risk scale. Give each one a mark:

0 = no risk to your health   **5 = very dangerous**

taking a bath	. . . .	flying	. . . .
taking a shower	. . . .	changing a light bulb	. . . .
eating in a restaurant	. . . .	watching TV	. . . .
kissing	. . . .	driving your car	. . . .
taking a walk	. . . .	going camping	. . . .
smoking	. . . .	hitch-hiking	. . . .

Does everyone in the class agree?

Reading

The following are real news headlines, followed by extracts from real newspaper articles. First, try to complete the headlines on your own before comparing with a partner:

a. . . . . FALLS ON MOVING CAR IN INDIANA,
KILLING TWO ADULTS AND THEIR TWO CHILDREN

b. MAN DIES AFTER BEING . . . . IN THE HEAD IN
NEW YORK CITY STREET

c. . . . . FATALLY STRIKES MAN IT WAS SENT TO HELP

d. JET-SKI OPERATOR DIES IN HIGH-SPEED COLLISION
WITH A . . . .

Now read the articles and then go back and correctly complete the headlines.

1. A dead tree fell on top of a passing car, crushing the passenger compartment and killing a minister, his wife and two of their children. "No wind. No storm. The chances of that tree falling at the time they were directly underneath it are astronomical," said Hancock County Sheriff Nick Gulling.

2. A man died after he was punched in the head by another man while walking along a New York City street, police said. Neil Eddelson, 39, and a friend were walking from a bar in Lower Manhattan's Tribeca neighbourhood around 9:30 pm on Wednesday. Another man approached, punched Eddelson in the head and ran off, police said.

3. An elderly man wandering in the street was struck and killed by a fire engine sent to help him, the authorities said. The fire engine was moving slowly when it struck the elderly man while he was out looking for the fire brigade. He died instantly.

4. A man dashing across a lake on his jet-ski at about 55 mph was killed in a collision with a flying duck. "Our theory is that the bird was in the air and hit him in the head," said David Bamdas, an owner of a boat dealership. The bird's carcass was found nearby and there were feathers on the jet-ski's handlebars, said the Broward County Sheriff's spokesman, Hugh Graf.

Discussion

Discuss these questions in pairs or small groups:

1. Were you surprised by any of these? Why/Why not?
2. Were all of these 'accidents' or 'unintentional'?
3. Could any of these have been easily prevented? How?

Language

Here are possible reactions to the four situations you read about. Which is the best natural reaction to each?

a. I don't believe it. It just sounds amazing!
b. What a coincidence! The odds of that happening must have been incredible.
c. That's incredibly sad.
d. How awful! I suppose there are mad people everywhere.

Notice these different ways to react to amazing news:

What a + noun:
What a coincidence!   What a terrible thing to happen.   What an awful thing to go through!

How + adjective:
How awful!   How amazing!   How incredible!   How unbelievable!

That's / That sounds + adjective:
That's amazing!   That's terrible!   That sounds awful!   That sounds unbelievable!

Complete the following situations using words from the examples above:

1. Did you hear that a little girl was killed by a falling tree today?
   > . . . . . . awful! How did it happen?

2. There's been a crash on the underground and a lot of people have been injured.
   > That . . . . . . terrible. I hope nobody's been killed.

3. A friend of mine was backing her car into her drive when she ran over her dog.
   > Oh, that's terrible! . . . . . . awful thing to have to tell your children!

4. There's been an earthquake in Turkey and thousands of people have lost their homes.
   > . . . . . . terrible! I hope it's nowhere near where your friends live.

5. Have you heard the news today? A guy ran amok and shot 6 people in a supermarket in Sydney.
   > . . . . . . appalling! You wonder what gets into these people.

6. Something terrible has happened this morning. There's been a gas explosion in town.
   > That . . . . . . terrible! Do they know how it happened yet?

Accidents in the home

Did you know that most injuries to people happen within the four walls of their own home? Here are some true statements about safety in the home. Can you complete them using the following words?

falling
children
kitchen
hospital
lethal

1. Almost 40% of all accidents which need . . . . treatment happen in people's homes.
2. Among the most dangerous rooms are the . . . . , the bedroom and the bathroom.
3. Almost 40% of all accidents in the home involve someone . . . .
4. The most serious danger in any home is fire. It spreads fast and is often . . . .
5. Accidents involving . . . . often occur in the presence of an adult.

Discussion

Discuss the following in pairs or small groups:

1. Do you believe the kinds of events discussed so far in this unit are pure misfortune, or do you believe in fate?
2. Do you believe your life is in danger at any time? In what ways?
3. How do you feel about living:
   a. in an area which has a recent history of violent earthquakes?
   b. in an area where hurricanes or cyclones are an annual occurrence?
   c. near an active volcano?
   Do you think people in these areas take 'a calculated risk' or don't they think about it?
4. Do you know anyone who likes to live dangerously? What do you think the term 'adrenaline junky' means? What sort of people are they?
5. *'It may be that your sole purpose in life is to serve as a warning to others.'*
   How do you feel about this remark? Could it be true – or just uncaring?

Survivors!

Discussion

With a partner, decide which three of these survival situations are the worst:

1. being lost at sea in a small yacht
2. travelling to do business in a country where you do not speak the language
3. losing your wallet, credit cards and passport in a foreign country
4. being lost in the middle of a forest
5. living in a dangerous part of the city where people are regularly mugged
6. having two fifteen-year-old nephews to stay for a weekend without their parents
7. being the only one at a party who doesn't know anyone
8. your car breaking down on the motorway

Reading

Read these newspaper articles and answer the questions below. Do you think you could have survived?

BOY USES BELT TO STOP BLEEDING

ABBEVILLE, S.C (AP) A boy whose leg was severed by a train used his belt to stop himself from bleeding to death – a skill he learned from his mother when she was studying to be a nurse.

Alex Compton, 10, was crossing the tracks near his home on Monday when his foot got caught on some rocks.

After the accident, he removed his belt and tightened it around his thigh to stop the bleeding, rescue workers said. He learned the technique from his mother, Lisa Compton, who had studied first aid at school. A neighbour found Alex beside the track. His leg was also found but doctors couldn't re-attach it.

Abbeville County Coroner Ronnie Ashley said he had never known anyone to survive such an accident. "Alex is a very, very brave child," Ashley said. "He's something special. He keeps wanting to know how he's going to ride his bicycle and how he is going to run and play with the other kids."

LOST MAN SURVIVES IN WOODS

GORMAN, Calif. (AP) A 25-year-old man who wandered into the Angeles National Forest a month ago and got lost has been found alive, police said.

Sean Kelly, who was reported missing on September 30th, was found by a hunter on Monday about 60 miles north of downtown Los Angeles, sheriff's Deputy Michael Lorenci said.

Kelly was too weak to walk, so rescuers transported him by helicopter to Henry Mayo Newhall Memorial Hospital, where he was treated.

Kelly told the hunter he had been lost for about two weeks and survived by eating roots and bugs, Lorenci said. To survive, he covered himself with dirt and branches at night to keep warm.

"We're all surprised that he'd been out there for 30 days and that he survived," Lorenci said. "It's not every day that something like this happens."

Work in pairs and mark the following statements:

    T = True   F = False   NEI = Not Enough Information

1. Alex Compton lost both legs.
2. If Alex Compton had not used his belt to stop the bleeding, he would have bled to death.
3. Alex Compton struggled to get to the hospital by himself.
4. Alex Compton has already come to terms with this incident.
5. Sean Kelly went into the woods to go camping.
6. Sean Kelly was forced to eat insects.
7. Sean Kelly was amazingly well after being so long in the woods.
8. Sean Kelly is an exceptionally lucky person to have survived such an experience.

Language

Look at this sentence from the second article:

It's not every day that something like this happens.

Does this mean that it is very unusual or that it is commonplace?

Divide the expressions below into those that mean 'very unusual' and those meaning 'more common':

	very unusual	more common
a. It was out of the ordinary.	☐	☐
b. It was a one-in-a-million chance.	☐	☐
c. It happens all the time.	☐	☐
d. It's hard to believe.	☐	☐
e. Imagine that!	☐	☐
f. It's not unheard of.	☐	☐
g. I think it's highly unlikely.	☐	☐
h. It's not the first time.	☐	☐
i. I'm not all that surprised.	☐	☐

Work in pairs. Use the above expressions to respond to the following:

1. Have you heard there's been an earthquake in central Turkey?
2. Someone's just been found alive after two months lost in Brazil.
3. There's been another bomb attack in Belfast.
4. There's been a massive pile-up on the M6 – nine people are known to have died.
5. Do you think the President will resign?
6. There's been a lot of flooding in Bangladesh.
7. All we need is one flake of snow and the trains are off!
8. They've found that girl who's been missing for six months – and she's alive and well!

Discussion

Work in pairs or small groups. Discuss the best ways to survive in these situations:

1. You are on holiday in Australia. You are swimming about a mile off shore. You have just seen a shark about 100 metres away.
2. The small plane you were travelling in has crashed in the middle of the jungle. You are unharmed, but you have no food or water.
3. You are in a busy street in the city. Buildings start moving. It's an earthquake!
4. You are on holiday – on safari in Africa. You are camping. A very large snake has entered your tent.
5. You wake up, smell smoke and realise that there is a fire in your house.
6. You are trapped in a crowded lift – 2 hours have passed and still no help has arrived.

We often read about people who lose their sight, their hearing, their speech, their sense of smell or taste. If you lost one of your senses, which would be the most difficult to cope without?

Do you spoil your kids?

Discussion

Discuss these questions with a partner:

1. Were you spoiled as a child?
2. What does 'spoiling' a child mean to you?
3. How many of the following things do you consider 'spoiling a child'?
   a. Giving a five-year-old pocket money.
   b. Taking a four-year-old child to Florida to see Disneyworld.
   c. Giving a child sweets every day.
   d. Letting a seven-year-old child stay up till 11 at night.
   e. Buying a child expensive toys.
   f. Sending a child to a private school.
   g. Buying a child the latest clothes.
   h. Letting a child watch as much television as he or she wants.

What other things do you consider spoil children?

Reading

Read the following article, then answer the questions which follow:

MICHAEL JACKSON DANGLES BABY OVER BALCONY

Berlin, Nov 20, 2002. Last night the singer Michael Jackson shocked his fans as he dangled his baby son over his fourth floor hotel balcony. It was not clear what Jackson's intentions were, but it looks as if he will escape a criminal investigation unless the German authorities receive a complaint from the general public.

It was ironic that the singer seemed to be putting his baby's life at risk while he was in the city to receive a lifetime achievement award and to attend a charity night for homeless children. In a written statement the singer said, "I made a terrible mistake. I got caught up in the excitement of the moment. I would never intentionally endanger the lives of my children."

The child, Prince Michael II, is Jackson's third and youngest. The boy, his tiny legs kicking, seemed to be covered with a white cloth as Jackson held him in mid-air from the luxurious Adlon Hotel.

Many people have aired doubts about Jackson's treatment of his three children. Whenever they appear in public, they wear masks so that nobody will recognise them. Jackson claims to be protecting them from exploitation by the media, but they seem to live in a private world, unable to mix with other children. Although their millionaire father will make sure they want for nothing, they are growing up with no mother present and incapable of going anywhere without the whole Jackson media circus in attendance.

Last year Jackson's father, Joseph, spoke out in favour of spanking children. He maintained that there wouldn't be so much crime if parents were prepared to punish their kids a little and take care that they stayed on the right track. Michael Jackson claims his father beat him and his brothers and sisters regularly when they were growing up.

1. Why did Jackson put his son's life at risk?
2. What is worrying about the way Jackson is bringing up his children?
3. What else do you know about Jackson and his children?
4. If you were rich and famous, how would you protect your children from the media?

Language

Work in pairs or small groups. Which of the following collocations to do with children have a negative connotation?

1. abuse a child
2. adopt a child
3. bring up a child
4. educate a child
5. indulge a child
6. look after a child
7. beat a child
8. discipline a child
9. raise a child
10. mistreat a child
11. neglect a child
12. spoil a child

Which of the above collocations describe these situations?

a. She's always giving in to that boy.
b. He taught me everything I know.
c. Where did you get those bruises?
d. They never say no.
e. They couldn't have any kids of their own, so …
f. She forgot to pick her up from school again.
g. That's it! Go straight to your room!

Discussion

Use this questionnaire first in pairs, then discuss it in the whole class:

What is your parenting style?

1. Your son asks you for a motorbike for his 18th birthday. You think they're dangerous.
   a. You buy him the motorbike.
   b. You offer to buy him a car on condition he gives up motorbikes.
   c. You tell him to forget about it.

2. Your 13-year-old daughter wants to go to the movies alone with a 16-year-old boy.
   a. You laugh and tell her to do her homework.
   b. You tell her OK, as long as her older sister goes with her.
   c. You let her go even though you don't agree with it.

3. You are the lucky winner of the state lottery – $50 million!
   a. You give your kids everything you never had.
   b. You make your kids struggle because you had to.
   c. You give them just what they need and no more.

4. Your 17-year-old son is going out on his first real date.
   a. You give him advice on safe sex.
   b. You give him your credit card and say, 'Have a great night!'.
   c. You ask him where he's going and offer him a lift and some cash.

5. Everyone in your daughter's class is getting tattooed. Your daughter, 18, wants to join the club. You don't like the idea.
   a. You tell her maybe, but you want to approve the design first.
   b. You absolutely forbid it.
   c. You reluctantly give her the money because you want her approval.

Do you drive?

Discussion

Discuss these questions in pairs or small groups:

1. Do you drive? If not, do you intend to take a driving test at some time?
2. What sort of car do you have? What sort of car would you like if you had the choice?
3. Do you think a person's car says something about them? If so, what?
4. Do you think you are a good driver? Why/Why not? What makes a good/bad driver?
5. Have you ever had an accident? What happened?

Reading

Read this article. Mark Mrs Dawkins' route on the map below and write in the names of the people who live at each house.

HOW NOT TO BE A GOOD NEIGHBOUR

68-year-old Elsie Dawkins had never had a driving lesson in her life. But when her husband, Reg, broke his leg and could not drive for six weeks, he asked her to start the car in order to charge the battery. If he had known what was going to happen, he might have acted differently.

Somehow, Mrs Dawkins put the car into reverse on the drive of their house at 17 Victoria Road, Worthing. The car shot backwards across the road and through Mr and Mrs Baker's front wall at number 18. In an attempt to correct the situation, Mrs Dawkins selected Drive in the two-year-old Peugeot 306 Automatic and set off again, leaving behind a trail of destruction. She careered over the road into the garden of number 15 and knocked down the fence between nos. 15 and 13. Narrowly missing the Volvo of Mike Taylor who lives at no.13, she smashed into the front garden of no. 11 and through a pond, luckily not killing any of the valuable koi carp that live there. At this point she managed to turn out on to the road but once again lost control, crashing into the gates in front of number 16, owned by Mr and Mrs Wheeler, and finally coming to a stop.

Daniel Hunt witnessed the whole event from his front room at no. 15. 'It was like something out of an old silent movie,' he said. 'I just could not believe what was happening. When she drove into Mrs Beecham's garden at number 11, I had begun to think it was quite funny and by the time she finally stopped I was laughing like hell.' Mrs Dawkins spent last night in Worthing General Hospital suffering from shock and minor injuries. She confessed to being extremely embarrassed and hoped that her neighbours would understand that it had all been a terrible accident.

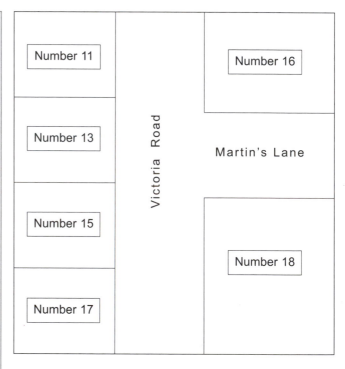

Discussion

Discuss these questions in pairs or small groups:

1. Do you think all Mrs Dawkins' neighbours felt the same way as Daniel Hunt?
2. How do you think some of them felt?
3. Do you think they will understand that 'it was all a terrible accident'?
4. What would you have done if you had been Daniel Hunt?
5. What do you think Mrs Dawkins will do when she gets out of hospital?
6. Do you know of anything like this ever happening in your country?

Language

1. Match the verbs on the left with an appropriate phrase on the right:

1.	start	a.	the battery
2.	have	b.	the gates
3.	charge	c.	on to the road
4.	put	d.	the car
5.	crash into	e.	the car into reverse
6.	turn out	f.	a driving lesson

Check your answers in the text.

2. Complete the text below with appropriate forms of expressions from the exercise above:

The day of my first driving test was the worst day I can remember! I was going to . . . . (1) first and then go on to take my test. My driving instructor arrived on time and we got into my car, but nothing happened. It was dead. I . . . . (2) and eventually managed to . . . . (3) . We set off and just arrived at the test centre in time. The examiner got into the car and asked me to drive out of the test centre car park. First of all I . . . . (4) and shot backwards about ten metres very suddenly. Then as I drove forwards . . . . (5), I . . . . (6) of the test centre. At that point the examiner said: 'If you don't mind, Mr Williams, I think it would be better if you came back another day.' I've never felt so humiliated.

Discussion

Answer the following questions on your own. Then compare your answers in pairs or small groups.

1. Speed cameras have just been installed in your town. Do you:
   a. drive more slowly all the time now?
   b. drive as usual, but slow down for the speed cameras because you know where they are?
   c. drive as usual – you always used to keep to the speed limit anyway.

2. You want to pick up a newspaper on your way to work but there isn't a parking space outside your local newsagent's. Do you:
   a. park illegally – you'll only be two minutes?
   b. go to a different newsagent's?
   c. wait till someone moves their car so you can park legally?

3. As you reverse out of a parking space you accidentally scratch the BMW parked next to you. Do you:
   a. drive off quickly?
   b. leave your name and address under the BMW's windscreen wiper?
   c. scratch the other side of the BMW too so it looks like vandalism?

4. You are in a hurry, driving along a twisting country road behind an old man and his wife who are going very slowly. Do you:
   a. try and overtake even though it might be quite dangerous?
   b. sound your horn to try and make the old fool let you past?
   c. find a radio station you like and relax – you'll only be five minutes late?

5. Someone accidentally, and quite gently, bumps into the back of your car at some traffic lights. You both get out of your cars. Do you say:
   a. 'You idiot! This car's only three weeks old'?
   b. 'I'll have your name and address, please. My garage'll be checking for any damage'?
   c. 'Doesn't look too bad to me but I reckon it's probably worth a drink'?

Special days and dates

Discussion

Work in pairs or small groups and discuss the following questions:

1. How many public holidays do you have in your country per year?
2. What sort of things do these holidays celebrate?
3. What do you do on these holidays?
4. Do you think the number of public holidays is too few, about right, or too many?

Compare your answers with another pair.

Did you know?

- The UK has fewer public holidays than any other European country.
- Before 1871 only Christmas Day and Good Friday were official holidays for everyone in Britain.
- There are now eight bank holidays in Britain.
- Northern Ireland has two extra days: March 17th (St Patrick's Day) and July 18th (the anniversary of the Battle of the Boyne).

Reading

Read the information below. Tick anything that you already knew:

Do you believe in coincidence?
Read this information about two great US Presidents.

- Abraham Lincoln was elected to Congress in 1846. John F. Kennedy was elected to Congress in 1946.
- Abraham Lincoln was elected President in 1860. John F. Kennedy was elected President in 1960.
- Andrew Johnson, who succeeded Lincoln, was born in 1808. Lyndon Johnson, who succeeded Kennedy, was born in 1908.
- John Wilkes Booth, who assassinated Lincoln, was born in 1839. Lee Harvey Oswald, who assassinated Kennedy, was born in 1939.
- Both Presidents were shot on a Friday.

But there's more than just coincidences about dates:
- Both Presidents were shot in the head.
- Both were particularly concerned with civil rights.
- Both were assassinated by Southerners.
- Both were succeeded by Southerners named Johnson.

- Lincoln's secretary was named Kennedy. Kennedy's secretary was named Lincoln.
- The names Lincoln and Kennedy each contain seven letters.
- Both assassins were known by their three names.
- Both names are composed of fifteen letters.
- Lincoln was shot at the theatre named Kennedy. Kennedy was shot in a Lincoln car.
- Booth ran from the theatre and was caught in a warehouse. Oswald ran from a warehouse and was caught in a theatre.
- Both Booth and Oswald were assassinated before their trials.
- A week before Lincoln was shot, he was in Monroe, Maryland. A week before Kennedy was shot, he was with Marilyn Monroe.

Read the information again and make a list of things which haven't been mentioned (because they obviously weren't coincidences). For example:

Kennedy didn't die exactly 100 years after Lincoln.
(In fact Lincoln died in 1865, Kennedy in 1963.)

Compare your answers in pairs or small groups.

How significant are the coincidences above? Are there any coincidences in your life?

Discussion

Many people born before about 1953 can remember exactly what they were doing when they heard that President Kennedy had been assassinated. Can you remember where you were and what you were doing when:

1. You heard that Princess Diana had been killed in a car crash in Paris.
2. You heard about the terrorist attacks on September 11th 2001.

What other events do you feel have had a similar impact?

Language

Complete the text below with words from the box:

procession	*fireworks*	*party*	*costumes*	*games*	*park*
band	*ceremony*	*church*	*festival*	*meal*	*homes*

Every year on 21st July our village has its own special . . . . (1). It is called the Festival of the Sea because the village is on the coast. The day starts with a . . . . . . (2) through the streets of the village. Everyone between the ages of 15 and 30 wears traditional . . . . (3) and there is a . . . . (4) which plays traditional music and songs. At about 12 o'clock everyone arrives at the . . . . (5) and there is a special . . . . (6) for the fishermen. After that, everyone goes back to their . . . . (7) for a special . . . . (8). Later, in the afternoon, everyone goes down to the . . . . (9) by the seafront. There are . . . . (10) for the children and the grown-ups play with the children and chat to each other. Then, when it starts to get dark, there are . . . . (11) and there is a big . . . . (12) with music and dancing. Everyone has a great time. Usually nobody gets to bed before about three in the morning – not even the children.

Discussion

Discuss the following in pairs or small groups:

1. Do you celebrate any of the following in your country?

   National Day
   Independence Day
   the longest / shortest day of the year
   either of the solstices (21st March, 21st September)
   name days

   What do you do on these days?

2. What religious festivals do you celebrate? What is the religious significance of these festivals? What happens on these days?

3. Are there other events, religious or otherwise, which you feel should be celebrated, either with or without a public holiday?

4. Your country has decided that there should be one more public holiday every year. Work in small groups and decide:

   when the holiday will be
   what it is going to celebrate
   what official celebrations (if any) there should be

5. What has been the most important day of your life so far?

Compare your answers with those of other groups.

Where do you live?

Discussion

Discuss these questions in pairs or small groups:

1. Where do you live?
2. What is your house like?
3. How long have you lived there?
4. Describe your favourite room.

Language

Match the words and phrases to the pictures:

treehouse   *wigwam*   *lighthouse*   *windmill*   *palace*   *log cabin*

Reading

Look at the three advertisements below. Answer these questions:

1. Which is the most expensive / cheapest?
2. Which is the biggest / smallest?
3. Which property needs some money spent on it?

THREE EXCEPTIONAL PROPERTIES FOR SALE

Built in 2000, this is a rare chance to acquire a truly fantastic treehouse with full living accommodation, set in beautiful countryside in south west Scotland. Kitchen/dining room, living room, four bedrooms, bathroom. Unbelievable! Price £90,000

Houseboat, Swan Island Harbour, River Thames. Two-bedroom floating home with 6m reception room and delightful river views. Heating with six electric radiators, hot water, roof garden, veranda, parking. These properties are rarely on the market. View now. Price: £230,000

French chateau near Poitiers, France. Set in a park, this magnificent property is built very much in the grand manner. It has 19 bedrooms, 24 other rooms, 2 towers, terraces and 65 hectares of parkland. In need of some modernisation. Price: £900,000

Discussion

Discuss these questions in pairs or small groups:

1. What do you think are the pros and cons of each of the three properties?
2. Which property do you think is the most unusual?
3. Have you ever seen or been in any properties like these? Where? What were they like?
4. Which would you most like to live in? Why?
5. Which would you least like to live in? Why?

Language

Use *house* or *home* to complete these sentences:

1. I hadn't met Sam before. He's great. We got on like a . . . . on fire.
2. I know the bridge looks a bit dangerous. But don't worry – it's as safe as . . . .
3. We stay at my sister's house so often – it's like a . . . . from . . . .
4. Yes, I suppose we had a good holiday. The weather was good but the hotel was nothing to write . . . . about.
5. No, no, put your wallet away. It's on the . . . .
6. Jamie, hi! Nice to see you. Come in! Make yourself at . . . .

Match each sentence above to the correct meaning below:

a. it was not very special
b. we liked each other
c. we are as happy as in our own home
d. it's very safe
e. be comfortable
f. it's free

Planning a house

Work in pairs. You want to build a house. You don't have enough money to build a house on your own, but you can manage it if you and your partner do it together. Plan the ideal house for both of you to live in together. Think about and discuss the points below and draw up a plan.

1. Where will it be? Will it have a view?
2. What style will it be in? Modern? Traditional?
3. What size will it be? How many rooms? How many floors?
4. How will it be decorated? Simply? Very traditionally? Plain colours? Flowery wallpaper?
5. Will it have a garden? What size? What style?
6. What about things like a swimming pool, sauna, tennis court?

Get together with other pairs and compare your designs.

Discussion

Work in pairs or small groups. What do you think the expressions below mean? Do you agree or disagree with them? Why?

1. Charity begins at home.
2. An Englishman's home is his castle.
3. There's no place like home.
4. Wherever I lay my hat, that's my home.
5. Home is where the heart is.

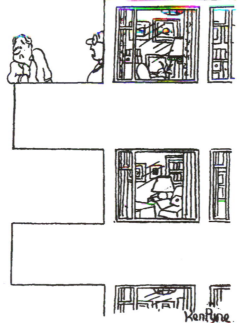

"On a clear day you can see the ground."

Unit by unit notes

1 Teenage rebellion

Reading

Elicit students' opinions on questions 1 – 3. Then read the texts about Ashley's view and the headmaster's view.

Answers:

1 Ashley was furious because they changed the colour of her hair in the photograph.

2 She thought the school should have given her a choice.

3 She had had pink hair since before Christmas.

4 He thought her hair did not bring credit upon her or the school.

5 He felt the school had acted reasonably by not excluding her and by allowing her to attend normal lessons.

Language

1 a. I went straight to the headmaster.
  b. I was just fuming.
  c. there is no way I'm …

2 a. We have been trying to resolve …
  b. Initially we were assured …
  c. … pupils are expected to bring credit upon themselves …
  d. We have not excluded Ashley from school. We have allowed her to attend normal lessons.

Possible answers:

1 I was extremely angry that he was unable to resolve the problem of the timetable.

2 I have no intention of ever allowing him into my classes.

3 I shall seek an immediate meeting with the director.

4 We have come to the decision that your son should be excluded from this school.

5 Initially I'd like to clarify that classes will take place as normal.

Protest

Elicit contemporary examples of youth culture from the students. Find out how they feel about the examples.

Bob Dylan was one of the most important singers of the 1960's. Note in the Dylan quotation 'agin' = 'ageing'. Ask the class why they think protest was so common at that time. What were the issues of the day? (the Vietnam War, women's rights, black rights, etc)

Can the class think of any pop lyrics today which shape the attitudes of young people?

You could ask the class to ask their parents what pop music was like when they were young. Were any of them part of the 60's generation?

2 Incredible stories

The stories in this unit can easily be added to from national and local papers or from the internet.

Reading

The stories 'Stuck in the Air' and 'Back Into The Records' are false:

Stuck in the Air

This story was reported by the BBC and other news agencies, but the airline later denied that it was true.

Back Into The Records

There is no guarantee that Ben Nevis has not been climbed by someone walking backwards!

Language 1

contestant, repetition, guidance, launch, operation, opponent, collection, ascent, descent.

Other possible nouns:

manager, contest, guide, operator, opposition, collector.

Language 2

1 contest
2 ascent
3 descent
4 collecting
5 repeated
6 manager
7 opponents
8 guidance

Discussion

You could display the stories around the classroom so that the class can read and discuss them all. Make sure that one person in each group is appointed to write the story down. Good groups should be able to work with 3 or 4 of the headlines. Weaker groups should do 1 and if they do that in a reasonable time, ask them to do another.

The cartoon

Why is the cartoon funny? You could put students into pairs to make up a story based on it. They must start: "Did you hear about the man who …"

3 Naming and shaming

Discussion
1b 2a 3f 4c 5h 6e 7d 8g

Reading
Make sure students know what 'stocks' are – a wooden structure which held a criminal's legs and arms so that they could not move. This was erected in a public place so that people could throw things at them, eg rotten eggs! A very old form of punishment in the UK – not used today!

1a The shoplifter had to walk up and down the street outside the shops he had stolen from with a sign that read: 'I am a thief. Do not steal. This could be you.'

1b The man had to write a one-dollar cheque every week to the man whose daughter he killed.

2 She thinks they will make people stop and think.

Discussion
If you wish, this activity could also lead into a discussion about what are appropriate punishments for schoolchildren.

Language
1 found guilty   6 committed
2 causing the death of   7 conviction
3 sentenced   8 criminal
4 fine   9 offenders
5 prison

He should be locked up/put behind bars/sent to prison.

At the end of the lesson, ask the class if they think naming and shaming is a suitable thing to do. Would it work in their culture?

4 Neighbours from hell

Reading
The Thompsons say that Miss Hill has:
- been unhelpful about keeping the shared drive clear
- stolen a strip of land when she replaced a fence
- cut down one of the Thompsons' trees
- allowed her dog to attack Mrs Thompson
- eaten the Thompsons' fish.

Language
1 a. disagreement, dispute, feud
  b. A 'feud' is a long-running argument. You can talk about a 'family feud'.

2 a. accuse, allege, claim
  b. claim
  c. because they give the idea that something may be true, but also that it may not be.

Expressions
1 dream
2 led
3 over
4 occasion
5 last
6 cause

Questionnaire
Ask students to do the questionnaire on their own before comparing their answers with a partner.

5 What's in a name?

You could start this discussion with the names of your class. Who has a common name? An unusual name? A nickname?

The origin of names
Cara - Celtic/Gaelic
Andrew - British
Pavel - Slavic
Fatima - Arabic
Tokala - Native American
Kunto - African
Meredith - Welsh
Duc - Vietnamese
Washi - Japanese
Chloe - Greek

Discussion
You could suggest that students try an internet site to find the most popular names for pets. Type in 'names for pets' and you will be surprised what you find – everything from thousands of name suggestions for your pet lizard to 'pet of the month' competitions! One of the main distinctions seems to be people who give their pets human names and those who give them 'fun' names.

6 You've got mail

True or false?
1 T   2 F   3 F   4 T

Language
1 visit a website
  go online
  surf the internet
  switch on your computer
  download music
  key in a password
  burn a CD
2 1 switch on   5 visit
  2 password   6 download
  3 go online   7 burn
  4 surf

Discussion

This is a good opportunity to bring in any current stories in the press relating to internet use or abuse. You could also raise the following topics:
- overall control of the internet
- to what extent parents should control their children's use of the internet
- should the police and governments exercise tighter control over material that is available on the internet?

7 Price and value

True or false?

1 F 2 T 3 F 4 T

Language

worth/costing a lot: valuable, extravagant, pricey, invaluable, expensive, exorbitant

worth/costing a little: cheap, inexpensive, economical

The following words are wrong:

1 expensive
2 exorbitant
3 valuable
4 pricey
5 economical
6 invaluable
7 pricey
8 cheap
9 valuable.

Discussion

a. £1,384,000
b. £10,000
c. £13,500
d. £28m
e. £30,000

8 Are we all criminals?

Reading

1 She took it and flew to France.
2 They took it to the local police station.

Language 1

1d 2c 3a 4b 5f 6e

Language 2

1 broke into
2 looking into
3 answered to
4 turned up
5 get away with
6 let (them) off

Discussion

In a multinational class you could ask students to discuss what kind of things are sometimes regarded as 'normal' in one country/culture but 'criminal' in another. For example: possessing firearms, non-payment of fines etc.

9 Things that go bump in the night!

Reading

1 The house that they bought is haunted, but they weren't told about this by the sellers.
2 A boy was strangled in the cottage in the late eighteenth century.
3 It is complete nonsense. She lived there for ten years and never had any problems.

Language

1 S 2 F 3 S 4 F 5 F 6 S

You could put pairs together into groups of four to discuss their ideas about 'it' in each sentence.

The cartoon

The cartoon is by Ken Pyne, one of the UK's most famous cartoonists. Do you think it is funny? Is it in bad taste? Why? Are there things we should not laugh at?

10 Living longer

Reading

1 They agree that ageing, and possibly even death, may no longer be inevitable.

2 There would be too many old people. This might mean that old people would need to be killed off to make way for younger people.

Discussion

'Generational cleansing' means getting rid of everyone of a particular generation. 'To clear away the dead wood' means to get rid of something (or in this case some people) that is no longer useful.

Language 1

a. medical science
b. life expectancy
c. the ageing process
d. life-threatening diseases
e. genetic engineering
f. the sanctity of human life

1 medical science
2 life expectancy
3 life-threatening diseases
4 genetic engineering
5 the ageing process

The cartoon
The cartoon is by Martin Honeysett, who specialises in drawing old people. Is this cartoon funny, sad, or does it contain some truth? Would old people find it funny?

11 Giving to charity

It might be useful to start this unit by listing important national and local charities in your country.

Reading
1 Pete, Brian (probably)
2 Michelle
3 Vikki

Discussion
1 Reasons for not giving (from the texts):
I'm not rich enough
Other people have more money than me.
We have to pay for things that used to be free.
I pay a lot of money in tax.

Language
1 giving (money) away
2 gave (it) back
3 giving out
4 give up
5 get (something) back
6 get by
7 pay back
8 got over

a get over
b get by
c give out
d give up

12 Jewellery for men

Reading
1 diamond jewellery
2 It is a way of showing everyone how rich he is.
3 A lot of men wear wedding rings.

Language
1 tiara	2 locket	3 necklace	4 earring
5 bracelet	6 brooch	7 chain	8 ring

13 Who cares about the environment?

Reading
1 A newspaper 2 c

1 Saving a very rare snail, protecting the world's smallest lizard (only recently discovered) and preserving the habitat of a rare flower

2 1,000 trees have been cut down to create a nature reserve for the snail; the lizard has been placed on the list of endangered species; important building work has been stopped.

3 He thinks there are more important things than these particular issues.

Language
1 b   2 f   3 a   4 e   5 c   6 d

14 The power of prayer

Prayer and religion are 'sensitive' areas about which people have strong and emotional views. Teachers should be careful which classes they use this material with and be sensitive to the feelings of all the students in the class.

Language
1 D   2 B   3 B   4 D   5 D   6 D   7 B   8 B   9 D
10 D

15 Revenge is sweet!

Reading
Note: a vicar is an Anglican priest.

The best headline is probably: VICAR CHEATS ON LOCAL DOCTOR

5 No. He had not intended to.
6 They went quiet.
7 She has left the area with the vicar.

The cartoon
Make sure students know the meaning of arson. Why do people normally commit arson?

Language
1 1   split up
  2   had an affair
  3   work out
  4   left
  5   get a divorce
  6   are together

2 1   went red
  2   was caught red-handed
  3   saw red
  4   paint the town red

16 A matter of birth and death

This can be a very sensitive issue. Treat it with care. It might be worth checking with a class in advance if this is a topic they would like to discuss.

Reading
1 F   2 T   3 F

Language
1 married
2 start
3 was
4 was expecting
5 gave
6 raised
7 fell
8 losing
9 adopt

17 Folk wisdom

Introduction
The first is a Chinese saying about the importance of education, practical skills and teaching people how to look after themselves. The second is a British saying that suggests that if there is a red sky in the evening, it will be a fine day the next day; whereas if there is a red sky in the morning, the weather will be bad. The first has some claim to wisdom; the second has no great claim to accuracy!

Reading
1 Murphy was a pessimist.
2 Things always go wrong.

Discussion
1 The writer *says* that Murphy's theories are of vital importance.
2 Not at all!

Discussion
1 have
2 grow
3 is
4 show
5 consists
6 see
7 has
8 Postpone

1 France
2 Native American
3 Iran
4 Germany
5 Norway
6 Japan
7 Spain
8 the Philippines

18 I'm on the train!

Reading
The writer thinks mobile phones are fantastic.

Discussion
1 The writer mentions the risks of being mugged (also of looking an idiot). Other potential risks concern the effects of radio waves on the brain, especially for young children.

Language 1
1 having no money
2 police
3 a stupid person
4 lavatory
5 alcohol
6 drunk
7 man
8 stole

Language 2
1 bloke/guy
2 plonker
3 pissed
4 booze
5 cops
6 nicked

The cartoon
What is the point of the two cartoons in this unit?

What is the second cartoon saying about people who beg in the street? Is this a valid or a cynical point of view?

19 Children and discipline

Reading
Jack Wallace thinks the laws are acceptable as they are now.
Jack Wallace was smacked as a child.
Laura Flynn would like to see all physical punishment banned.
Laura Flynn thinks smacking has more than a physical effect.

Language
1b 2d 3f 4h 5a 6c 7e 8g

Discussion
The discussion could be extended by asking how attitudes to children change from generation to generation.

20 Ever eaten dog?

This can, of course, be a sensitive issue if you have students from dog-eating countries in your class.

Reading
1 The writer ate dog.
2 Because he/she had to write an article about it.
3 He/She enjoyed it but wouldn't do it again.

True or false?
1 F 2 T 3 F 4 F

Language

a + delicious, + appetising, + tasty, - disgusting,
  - inedible, + mouth-watering, - bland, - tasteless

b - fatty, - tough, +/- sweet, - bitter, - rich,
  +/- spicy, - sour, - oily

3 a tough b oily c bitter d bland e sour

Discussion

2 deep fried tarantula = Cambodia
  chocolate-dipped scorpion = California
  grasshopper marinated in soy sauce = Japan
  deep fried ants = Colombia
  cockroach kebab = Burma
  termites fried in tomato = South Africa

21 A healthy lifestyle

Reading

a Angela M
b Andrew C

True or false?

1 F 2 F 3 T 4 T 5 T 6 F

Language

Cross out:

1 major   2 partially   3 bread

4 poor health

5 healthy environment

6 disgustingly healthy

7 healthy diet

8 excellent

22 Public figures, private lives

Reading

1 T   2 F   3 F   4 F

Discussion

1 The writer doesn't seem to like them much
  – he calls them 'ugly old journalists'.

2 Students' own answers.

3 'He is not usually unhappy about seeing his
  name in the papers.'

4 Students' own answers.

5 He doesn't seem against it – in fact he is
  curious about who Natasha Davies' companion
  was.

6 Students' own answers.

The cartoon

Ask students who the 'William' of the cartoon is.
This could lead to a discussion of the problems of
growing up in the public eye or it could lead to a
discussion of William's mother, Princess Diana,
and the way the press hounded her – some might
say, to her eventual death.

Language

Cross out:

1 partial   2 open   3 broad   4 abolish

1 business relationship

2 destroyed his reputation

3 established a reputation/a growing reputation

4 broke off the relationship

5 poor reputation

6 established a reputation

7 maintain a (good) relationship

8 casual relationship

23 Holidays from hell!

Language

1 in the hope of

2 in the first place

3 to catch a cold

4 a lack of sympathy

5 by no means

6 to spoil a holiday

7 all over the place

8 to deserve sympathy

1 by no means

2 in the hope of

3 to spoil a holiday

4 all over the place

5 to catch a cold

6 deserved (any) sympathy

7 lack of sympathy

8 in the first place

24 The dating game

Reading

Make sure all students know that GSOH means
'a good sense of humour'.

1 She has put an ad in a 'Lonely Hearts' column.

2 Because she finds it difficult to meet single men.

True or false?

1 T   2 F   3 F   4 T   5 T

Language

Possible answer (there are many possible ones):

1 Mark fancied Lucy.

2 He asked her out on a date.

3 They got on very well.

4 They started going out together.

5 They fell in love with each other.

6 Mark proposed to Lucy.

7 They got engaged.

8 They got married.

9 They went on their honeymoon.

10 Lucy became pregnant.

11 She had twin girls, Emma and Katie.

12 Mark and Lucy started to have rows.
13 Mark had an affair.
14 They split up.
15 Lucy asked for a divorce.
16 Lucy got custody of the children.

Discussion
You could ask students to bring in some ads from their own newspapers and translate them.

25 Newspapers

Reading
1 She almost drowned, but had a lucky escape.
2 Her teacher, Denise Carter.

Language 1
1 e 2 a 3 d 4 b 5 c

Discussion
1 the first
2 the first – human interest
3 the first
4 the second
5 the second
6 the second is concerned with news; the first with human interest
7 the first is probably from a tabloid newspaper; the second from a 'quality' paper
8 students' own answers

Language 2
1 horoscope
2 obituary
3 crossword
4 proprietor
5 TV guide
6 sports
7 headline, article
8 reviews
9 editor

26 To tip or not to tip?

In Britain it is customary to tip taxi drivers and waiters. Occasionally one may tip hairdressers, hotel porters and chambermaids. For taxi drivers and waiters the average tip is 10–12.5% of the total bill. For hairdressers and chambermaids the sum is discretionary. Often in restaurants a service charge is added to the bill, in which case it is not necessary to leave a further sum of money.

Language
1 decent
2 safe
3 tight
4 change
5 point
6 matter
7 break
8 nose

What do you say?
In Britain people commonly say: 'Thanks for everything' or 'Keep the change' or 'Here you are and thank you very much.'

27 Royalty

True or false?
1 T 2 T 3 F 4 T 5 F

NB: strangling pheasants is an act of mercy administered to pheasants which have been shot but not killed, when the Queen goes on a pheasant shoot.

Language
appoint a minister; elect a government; found a republic

opinion poll, election campaign, royal family, personal wealth

1 opinion poll
2 royal family
3 personal wealth
4 found a republic
5 elect a government
6 election campaign
7 appointed a prime minister

28 Fashion

Reading
What people wear and don't wear today 2
What fashion designers do 3
A very special dress 1

Questions in pairs
1 bright red ostrich feathers
2 2,000 shiny red glass beads
3 T-shirt and jeans
4 casual clothes (they dress down)
5 one other
6 nobody
7 many people think they are self-indulgent
8 as art

Language
Cross out: factory, leave

1 went out of
2 high
3 is (always) in
4 street
5 come back into
6 passing

29 Is it right to eat meat?

Reading
a the first
b the second
c the first
d the second

Language
1 For example
2 the way I look at it is this, Sure (that's understandable) but
3 Of course
4 what's more
5 Anyway

The cartoon
Make sure students know the meaning of protective colouring. You could use the cartoon to remind them that some nouns in English can be both countable and uncountable. For example:

I love feeding the pigeons.
I love pigeon.

The first example refers to the birds; the second refers to them as meat.

30 The exploitation of animals

This can be a sensitive issue if there are students in your class from countries where bullfighting is a popular sport.

Reading
Text 1 is in favour of bullfighting
Text 2 is against it.

Questions in pairs
1 Survival and domination of the wild.
2 As national heroes.
3 It is becoming more popular because it is a celebration of a uniquely national tradition.
4 They are kept in darkness so they are blinded by the sunlight when they come out into the bullring.
5 By using their horns.
6 No. Often they become tired. Sometimes the final 'death blow' does not kill them.
7 Yes.
8 Horses are sometimes attacked by the bulls; sometimes their vocal cords are cut out so their cries cannot be heard by the crowd.

Language
1 stick
2 listen
3 misunderstood
4 something
5 minute
6 point
7 interrupt
8 clearly
9 another
10 take

To correct someone you might use: 1, 3, 6, 8, 9.

To make a positive contribution you might use: 4, 5, 7, 10.

Number 2 is rude. Others may sound rude depending on your tone of voice.

31 Why get married?

Be sensitive to students' feelings about using this unit. If any students in your class are recently divorced or separated, it might be better to choose a different topic. The first page of this unit is a light-hearted look at the topic.

Reading
1 Several thousand dollars
2 He says he hasn't found the right person yet.
3 Because they thought they'd all be bachelors for a long time.
A 'confirmed bachelor' is a man who has decided never to marry.

Language
1	A	12	B
2	B	13	A
3	B	14	B
4	B	15	B
5	A (B)	16	B
6	B	17	A
7	B	18	A
8	B	19	A
9	A (B)	20	B
10	A	21	B
11	A	22	A

32 I hate my boss!

Language
1 sick 2 take 3 break 4 with 5 enough 6 stand

33 Scams – how can people be so stupid?

Reading
1 Perhaps in his 50's or 60's.
2 Possibly a company sold him something which was a waste of money.
3 It means 'very easy'.

Part 1
1 Students' own answers
2 They met at bingo.

Part 2
3 Because she realised it was her last chance to get any of Mr Stockton's money.
4 Altogether, over $55,000
5 None
6 Students' own answers

Language
Dialogue 1: been had
Dialogue 2: talked me into
Dialogue 3: fell for
Dialogue 4: taken in by

Discussion
It is very easy to find scam websites on the internet – eg pet funerals.

The cartoon
Make sure students know what gerbils are. Ask them why the family had so many gerbils. What was the scam? *(It is common in the UK for children to be sent home at the end of a party with a 'party bag' full of things like sweets. The joke partly depends on students knowing that the children have been given an unwanted gerbil instead of a party bag! How will their parents react?)*

34 Bad habits

Discussion
1 It stank and housed rats.
2 There was 154 tons of rubbish.
3 No – some were still alive.
4 They had 'a soft spot' for them.
5 Possibly – it's not clear from the article.
6 Up to 6 feet long (about 1.82m)

Language
1 bite your nails
2 crack your knuckles
3 grind your teeth
4 pick your nose
5 snap your fingers
6 play with your hair

Discussion
(possible answers)

1 smoking
2 drinking
3 nail biting
4 nose picking
5 TV addict
6 surfing
7 hoarding
8 shopping
9 eating sweets/chocolate

35 Killed by a flying duck!

Reading
Possible answers:
a rock / tree
b shot / punched
c ambulance / police car / fire engine
d shark / swimmer / whale / boat

Actual answers:
a tree   c fire engine
b punched   d flying duck

Language
Possible reactions:
a = headline 1b   c = headline 3c
b = headline 2d   d = headline 4a
1 How
2 's / sounds
3 What an
4 How
5 How
6 's / sounds

For more information on unusual ways that people die, visit: www.darwinawards.com

Accidents in the home
1 hospital
2 kitchen
3 falling
4 lethal
5 children

36 Survivors!

Be careful about using this unit if any members of the class are particularly squeamish!

Reading
1 F 2 T 3 F 4 NEI 5 NEI 6 T 7 T 8 T

Language
Suggested answers:
1h 2b or e 3i or h 4h 5d or g 6h 7c or i
8b or e

37 Do you spoil your kids?

Reading
1 He said he got caught up in the excitement of the moment.
2 They wear masks in public; they don't mix with other children; they have no mother; wherever they go they are accompanied by the whole Jackson entourage.
3 Students' own answers
4 Students' own answers

Language
negative ideas are: 1, 5, 7, 10, 11, 12
a indulging a child
b educating a child
c beating/mistreating/abusing a child
d indulging/spoiling a child
e adopting a child
f neglecting a child
g disciplining a child

38 Do you drive?

Reading

The following is a rough sketch of what happened:

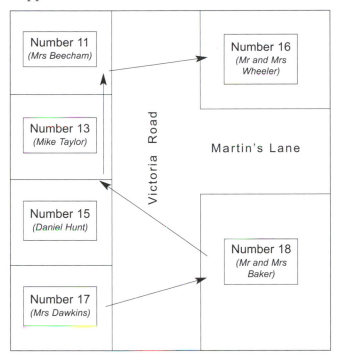

Language

1 start the car
2 have a driving lesson
3 charge the battery
4 put the car into reverse
5 crash into the gates
6 turn out on to the road

1 have a driving lesson
2 charged the battery
3 start the car
4 put the car into reverse
5 turning out on to the road
6 crashed into the gates

39 Special days and dates

Discussion (second page)

The death of Princess Diana was important in Britain and in France, where it happened. Ask students if she is remembered in their country. Perhaps they remember the death of someone important in their country. If so, who?

Language

1 festival
2 procession
3 costumes
4 band
5 church
6 ceremony

7 homes
8 meal
9 park
10 games
11 fireworks
12 party

40 Where do you live?

Language

1 lighthouse
2 log cabin
3 wigwam
4 treehouse
5 windmill
6 palace

Reading

1 The French chateau is the most expensive; the treehouse the cheapest.
2 The chateau is the biggest; the houseboat the smallest.
3 The chateau needs money spent on it – it is 'in need of some modernisation'.

Language

1 house
2 houses
3 home/home
4 home
5 house
6 home

1b   2d   3c   4a   5f   6e

The cartoon

Ask students what kind of building is in the picture. Would they like to live in that kind of high-rise block? On the 10th floor? Or the 30th?